Rodrigo
Gmez T.

TIMES ALONE

TIMES ALONE

○~○○~○○~○○~○○~○○~○○~○○~○○~○○~○○~○○~○○~○○~○

SELECTED POEMS OF
ANTONIO MACHADO

○~○○~○○~○○~○○~○○~○○~○○~○○~○○~○○~○○~○○~○○~○

CHOSEN AND TRANSLATED BY

ROBERT BLY

WESLEYAN UNIVERSITY PRESS

MIDDLETOWN, CONNECTICUT

Acknowledgments:
The translator is grateful to the editors of the following journals, who pub-
lished some of these translations: *Tennessee Poetry Journal, Ironwood, Michi-
gan Quarterly, Doones, Creative Arts Journal, The Nation, Massachusetts
Review, White Pine Press, River Styx, Plainsong,* and the *Harvard Advocate.*

A few of the poems were also published earlier in three chapbooks: *Canciones,*
Toothpaste Press; *I Never Wanted Fame,* Ally Press; *Times Alone,* Copper
Canyon Press.

All inquiries and permissions requests should be addressed to the Publisher,
Wesleyan University Press, 110 Mt. Vernon Street, Middletown, Connecticut
06457

Distributed by Harper & Row Publishers, Keystone Industrial Park, Scranton,
Pennsylvania 18512

LIBRARY OF CONGRESS CATALOGING IN PUBLICATION DATA

Machado, Antonio, 1875–1939.
    Times alone.

    English and Spanish.
    1. Bly, Robert.   II. Title.
    PQ6623.A3A243   1983   821'.62   83–6955
    ISBN 0–8195–5087–6
    ISBN 0–8195–6081–2 (pbk.)

Manufactured in the United States of America
First Edition

to James Wright
(1927–1980)

Making things well
is more important than making them
(A. Machado)

CONTENTS

TIMES ALONE

A FEW NOTES ON
ANTONIO MACHADO

ANTONIO MACHADO is the most thoughtful, modest, and lovable poet of the twentieth century. His quiet labor on sound and rhythm over many years, his emphasis on the suffering of others rather than his own, the passageways that he creates inside his poems that lead back to the ancient Mediterranean past, his inner calm, even joyfulness—all of these gifts nourish people wherever he is read.

* * *

His poetry secretes in itself the rhythm of the walker. When John Dos Passos, just out of college, traveled to see Machado in Segovia, he found an awkward man with a deep voice, "an old-fashioned teacher," dressed in a black double-breasted suit, who walked for hours in Segovia and the countryside. When a person walks, he experiences objects one by one at a pace agreeable to the body. And every walk ends; sooner or later the walk is over and we are back home.

* * *

Yeats connected true poetry with trance. And when Lorca says:

> *one day . . . the enraged ants*
> *will throw themselves on the yellow skies that have*
> *taken refuge in the eyes of cows*

we fall into a trance immediately. But Machado has vowed not to soar too much; he wants to "go down to the hells" or stick to the low and ordinary: flies, blind mules working the water wheels, stony earth, dogs, old men who stare straight ahead for hours astonished by nothing, boring schoolrooms, unsolvable philosophical problems. How does he help the reader to fall into a trance then? By his vowel sounds, exquisite, astonishing, magical, and by his care in measuring time inside the line. Sometimes a hypnotist swings a watch; Machado does that: the beats return regularly, the vowels come again, time passes so slowly it can be measured; we listen. The trance of ordinary life, chaotic, gives way to an ordered trance, and water goes on flowing while we are asleep. Perhaps water flows best in the river while we are asleep. Water through the fountain lifts itself in the air. But we are asleep.

* * *

Machado had an answer to what poetry is: "la palabra en el tiempo." We could translate this cryptic phrase as: "the word in time," "human language in which we feel time passing," or "words that pick up the energy of time," or "words that take their place, like drumbeats, in time already counted." He loved to get a phrase like "la palabra en el tiempo" and repeat it until no one could understand what it meant. Of course he adored narrative in poems, which contains time as a jar of water contains water.

And doesn't form move through time? "A Chinese jar still moves perpetually in its stillness." Doesn't a snail develop its gorgeous logorhythmic shell-curve by moving through time? We could say that only when the snail agrees not to be eternal, when it accepts the descent into earth time that unfolds slowly, only then does the snail achieve that form which we foolishly associate with eternity. Machado adored the well-made thing:

> *Form your letters slowly and well:*
> *making things well*
> *is more important than making them.*

* * *

One of the first poems of Machado's that attracted me was his poem on the bean fields, which I saw in 1959 in Willis Barnstone's translation:

> *The blue mountain, the river, the erect*
> *coppery staffs of slender aspens,*
> *and the white of the almond tree on the hill.*
> *O flowering snow and butterfly on the tree!*

With the aroma of the bean plants, the wind
runs in the joyful solitude of the fields!

We feel that Machado is laying a relatively light hand on nature here. I was more accustomed to poems in which the author uses nature to make philosophical points: What a certain ape did is brought in to bolster an argument, the swan sailing becomes a symbol of pride, the snake is either evil or wisdom, but seldom a real snake. John Donne writes well, but his fleas always seem to fit into some elaborate human system, alchemical, Christian, or occult. There is nothing the matter with that, except that we may not have asked the snake or the flea how he feels about it.

It seems that in the West, in general, when we write about a field, we bring the field into our study and close the door. Not all poets do, of course. But one feels that Machado doesn't ask the field to come to his poem, but he brings his poem to the bean field . . . and even more amazing, he leaves it there!

With the aroma of the bean plants, the wind
runs in the joyful solitude of the fields!

That doesn't mean that Machado is a nature Romantic; (he is in fact suspicious of the Romantics;) nor that he undervalues the intellect; (he took in fact his advanced degree in philosophy). I think it means that he wishes to give to the fields a respect similar to the respect he gives to an idea.

* * *

His favorite philosopher was Pythagoras. Pythagoras appears in his poetry from beginning to end. Pythagoras' doctrine of the "music of the spheres" is probably present, along with God, in the early poem:

It's possible that while sleeping the hand
that sows the seeds of stars
started the ancient music going again

—like a note from a great harp—
and the frail wave came to our lips
as one or two honest words.

[3]

Pythagoras gave him confidence to write brief poems, for Pythagoras left only sayings. And yet his sayings suggest a secret bond between the "sower of the stars," and the lyre-player on earth. We see a gesture of someone sowing grain, whose hand sweeps the strings of a lyre, and from it comes a wave of music that reaches even to Spain. When Spain lost the remains of her empire in 1898, the writers of that generation realized that the old rhetorical bluff was over, and they had to live now with reduced expectations, a diminished thing, sadness, grief, limited resources, a few words that were honest.

*   *   *

Reading Machado, one is moved by his firm and persistent efforts to see and to listen. He does not want to be caught as the narcissist is, in an interior world, alone with his consciousness, but he wants to cross to other people, to the stars, to the world:

> *To talk with someone,*
> *ask a question first,*
> *then—listen.*

Daydreaming is not useful for crossing, but eyes are. "Today, just as yesterday, the job of the eyes, the eyes in the head and in the mind, is to see." The landscape around Soria he studies with fierce attention. How to study the outer world without losing inward richness—that is the issue Rilke and Ponge lived. If we look only at our problems, Machado said, the inner world dissolves; if we look only at the world, it begins to dissolve. If we want to create art, we have to stitch together the inner world and the outer world. How to do that? Machado concludes, well, we could always use our eyes.

One of his earliest memories, which he included in Juan de Mairena's notebooks, is this: "I'd like to tell you the most important thing that ever happened to me. One day when I was still quite young, my mother and I were out walking. I had a piece of sugar cane in my hand, I remember—it was in Seville, in some vanished Christmas season. Just ahead of us were another mother and child—he had a stick of sugar cane too. I was sure mine was bigger—I knew it was! Even so, I asked my mother—because children always ask questions they already know the answer to: 'Mine's bigger, isn't it?' And she said, 'No, my boy, it's not. What have you done with your eyes?' I've been asking myself that question ever since."

The Ch'an teachers tell a story about a man of the world who one day confronts a master, and asks him to sum up what he has learned in his life as a Buddhist monk. The master hands him a piece of paper with one word written on it: "Attention!" The worldly man now insists that he is a serious student, and implies that the master is holding back. He takes the paper back and writes "Attention. Attention." The worldly man now appeals to the master's humanity, points out that he too has a soul, and they will both die soon; it is the master's duty to tell him what he needs to know. The master says: "You're right." Taking the paper he writes three words: "Attention! Attention! Attention!" Much of Machado's life he spent in this effort of attention.

* * *

Machado in his work makes clear that we in the West have our own tradition of attention. Pythagoras, for example, listened to vibrations. He usually began a lecture with the monochord, which he plucked so that his listeners could hear the note clearly; then, breaking the string at its nodes, he let them hear the overtones. He then pointed out that the relationships between the vibrations they had just heard corresponded to the relationships between the speeds of the planets. Paying attention, in the tough sense of the phrase, means paying attention to nonhuman vibrations, the life of cat-gut and planets. Pythagoras said, "When you get up in the morning, smooth out the shape of your body from the bed."

When Machado pays attention, he pays attention to time, which surely existed before human beings; to landscape, whose rhythm Machado said is slower than human rhythm; to the past of each city he lived in, for each city's life extends beyond our individual life; to the way colors unfold (Goethe studied color also); to synchronicity, that is occasional identity of human and natural events; and to the curious world of dreams. "Pythagoras' lyre goes on resonating in dreams," he said. Yet he did not want to lose "we". He knew that a secret "you" was present in the feelings evoked by a landscape. In poetry every feeling, he said, "needs for its creation the distress of other frightened hearts among a nature not understood. . . . In short, my feeling is not only mine, but *ours*."

* * *

Antonio Machado was born on July 26, 1875, in Seville. Until he was eight, he lived in the enormous Palacio de las Dueñas, where his father, a teacher and early collector of folk poetry and folk music in Spain, lived as a kind of caretaker for the Duke of Alba. It had long passageways. When Antonio was eight, the family moved to Madrid; there Antonio and his brothers attended the Free Institution of Learning, whose founder, Francisco Giner de los Ríos, had a profound effect on two or three generations of Spanish intellectuals and writers. Antonio tended to be torpid and slow; he took ten extra years to get his B.A. He published his first book when he was twenty-eight. Eventually he chose a career as secondary-school teacher of French, passed the examination, and when he was thirty-two got his first job at Soria, a poor and exhausted town in the grazed-out mountainous area of Castile. He stayed there five years. During the second year he married the daughter of the family in whose pension he lived, Leonor, then fifteen. He watched her sicken of tuberculosis and die after two more years, in the fall of 1911. "She is always with me," he said; he addressed her often in later poems, and never remarried. He abandoned the idea of suicide, with arguments rather like Frost's: He wrote to Jiménez that he did not want to annihilate whatever in him was helpful and constructive. He resigned his position at Soria, and transferred to Baeza, in the south, nearer his first home, and stayed there seven years. During 1912, his last year in Soria, his second book, *The Countryside of Castile*, came out; and he continued to add

[6]

poems to it during his years in Baeza. In 1919, he transferred again, this time to Segovia, which is only an hour from Madrid. He was able now on weekends to escape from provincial life, which he complained was boring and deadening; and he began writing plays and taking part in the intellectual life of Madrid. He lived in Segovia from 1919 to 1932, thirteen years, during which he fell in love with a married woman he called "Guiomar," invented two poet-philosophers named Abel Martín and Juan de Mairena, and published his third book, *Nuevas canciones* (*New Poems*). He became more and more active in public life, writing in the papers on political and moral issues during the exciting period that led in 1931 to the proclamation of the Second Spanish Republic. He lived in Madrid after 1932 with his brother José and wrote, disguised playfully as Juan de Mairena, many articles in the newspapers defending the Republic and its plans. After the civil war began in 1936, he continued to write prose, but little poetry, and finally, January 28, 1939, moving ahead of Franco's army, crossed the Pyrenees as a passenger in an old car, holding his mother on his lap. He died at Collioure, just over the border, on February 22, and as the gravestones make clear, his mother survived him by only a few days. His attitude toward his own life resembled James Wright's toward his: that it was a bookish life, and the events were not too important.

* * *

What about liveliness? Everything is to be lively. When he was living at Segovia, he began to feed his made-up philosopher Juan de Mairena bits of prose that he had written earlier. Here is a little scene:

"Mr. Pérez, please go to the board and write:
The daily occurrences unfolding on the avenue."
The student did as he was told.
"Now go ahead and put that into poetic language."
The student, after some thought, wrote:
What is going on in the streets.
"Not bad!"

So Machado, though he wanted poetry to have nobility and beauty, refused to achieve that through poetic or archaic language, which he knew involved a misuse of time.

"Mr. Martínez, go to the board and write:
    Those olden swords of the glorious times. . ."
The student obeyed.
"To which time do you think the poet was alluding here?"
"To the time when the swords were not old."

"Every day, gentlemen, literature is more 'written' and less spoken. The result is that every day we write worse, in a chilly prose, without grace, however correct it may be: our eloquence is merely the written word fried again, in which the spoken word has already been encased. Inside every orator of our time there is always a clumsy journalist. The important thing is to speak well: with liveliness, thought, and grace. The rest will be given us as a gift."

He distrusts ancient eloquence:

"The truth is the truth,"—perhaps Agamemnon said it or his swineherd.
Agamemnon: "Absolutely clear."
Swineherd: "I'm not sure about that. . . ."

FROM

TIMES ALONE
PASSAGEWAYS IN THE HOUSE
AND OTHER POEMS

SOLDEDADES

GALERÍAS

Y OTROS POEMAS

FIRST EDITION 1903

ENLARGED IN 1907

ANTONIO MACHADO wrote some of his dream poems in his first book, *Soledades*, in 1899; Freud published his *Interpretation of Dreams* the same year. Machado independently makes dreams a primary subject of his poems, descends into them, looks to them for guidance, goes downward, farther and farther until he finds water. The water he has found makes *Soledades* refreshing. One could say that "the world" exerts tremendous pressure on the psyche, collective opinion terrorizes the soul; the demands of the world obsess the pysche, and the world and its attractions offer to use up all the time available. Each person needs then, early on, to go inside, far enough inside to water the plants, awaken the animals, become friends with the desires, and sense what Machado calls "the living pulse of the spirit," start the fire in the hearth, and close the door so that what is inside us has sufficient power to hold its own against the forces longing to invade. Machado has achieved this inner strengthening by the time he finishes his first book, and his praise of dreams is clear:

> *Memory is valuable for one thing,*
> *astonishing: it brings dreams back.*

His deep-lying confidence he perhaps received as a reward for his labor, or perhaps it was given as a gift; we can't tell. But the confidence is unmistakable:

> *There the good and silent spirits*
> *of life are waiting for you,*
> *and one day they will carry you*
> *to a garden of eternal spring.*

> * * *

> *But She will not fail to come.*

[11]

In the golden poplars
far off, the shadow of love is waiting for you.

It's clear that his confidence rises from some source far below the intellect, far below even the security provided by the healthy mind in the healthy body. This sort of confidence seems to spring from earliest infancy. The positive, energetic mother holds the child near her heart, and he looks out on the world: it seems all blossoming, all good, and he carries that confidence with him all his life. Machado suggests that if he were a Provençal love poet, and wrote a poem to a woman's eyes, it would probably go this way:

> *your clear eyes, your eyes have*
> *the calm and good light,*
> *the good light of the blossoming world, that I saw*
> *one day from the arms of my mother.*

Even though *Soledades* is the book of a young man, he asks questions in it usually not asked until old age. One poem begins:

> *Faint sound of robes brushing*
> *the exhausted earth!*

This is not a romantic poem about village life, as I first thought: he says that if one really wants to be depressed, one can listen to this sound—the Spanish priest's robe brushing worn-out soil. It reminds us of Blake's despair in London. Machado warns us that we are not alone:

> *Snowy Roman ghosts*
> *go about lighting the stars.*

And he warns that in such situations, it is very easy for "a phantasm" to come, and throw off our sense of reality.

And he asks hard questions about what is going on inside. What if we, out of fear or recklessness or carelessness have stopped the soul's growth? What if we, having invited the world to be with us, have let the life of the feeling die?

The wind, one brilliant day, called
to my soul with an aroma of jasmine.

"In return for this jasmine odor,
I'd like all the odor of your roses."

"I have no roses; I have no flowers left now
in my garden. . . . All are dead."

"Then I'll take the waters of the fountains,
and the yellow leaves, and the dried-up petals."

The wind left. . . . I wept. I said to my soul,
"What have you done with the garden entrusted to you?"

When we have finished the book, we are aware that Machado has found certain passageways that lead inward or certain paths that lead downward, and they are not collective paths; and because he has found those paths, on his own, it doesn't matter so much if he is successful or not, if his life is full or not.

Kabir ended one poem:

If you want the truth, I'll tell you the truth;
Friend, listen: the God whom I love is inside.

Kabir says that simply and flatly, with his entire culture behind him. Machado calls out in a magnificent poem, parallel to Kabir's, a similar vision, and calls his vision a "marvellous error."

Last night, as I was sleeping,
I dreamt—marvellous error!—
that I had a beehive
here inside my heart. . . .

Last night, as I slept,
I dreamt—marvellous error!—
that it was God I had
here inside my heart.

The Westerner, after centuries of extroverted science, and determined philosophical attempts to remove soul from conversation, architecture, observation and education, sees inside himself, and sees what the ancients saw, but can hardly believe it. He confesses that he must be seeing wrong.

In 1917, when Machado put together his *Selected Poems*, he wrote an introductory piece for *Soledades*, and this is what he said:

The poems of this first book, which was published in January of 1903, were written between 1899 and 1902. Around that time, Rubén Darío, whom the critics then in fashion attacked with mockery, was the idol of a small minority. I too admired the author of *Prosas profanas (Worldly Stories)*, the great master of form and feeling, who later revealed the depth of his soul in *Cantos de vida y esperanza (Poems of Life and Hope)*. But I tried—and notice I do not boast of results, but only of intentions—to follow a quite distinct road. I thought that the substance of poetry does not lie in the sound value of the word, nor in its color, nor in the metric line, nor in the complex of sensations, but in the deep pulse of the spirit; and this deep pulse is what the soul contributes, if it contributes anything, or what it says, if it says anything, with its own voice, in a courageous answer to the touch of the world. And I thought also that a man can overtake by surprise some of the phrases of his inward conversations with himself, distinguishing the living voice from the dead echoes; that he, looking inward, can glimpse the deep-rooted images, the things of feeling which all men possess. My book was not the systematic realization of this proposal, but such were my artistic intentions at that time.

This book was republished in 1907, with the addition of new poems which added nothing substantial to the original work, under the title *Soledades, galerías y otros poemas*. The two volumes in effect made up a single book.

ANTONIO MACHADO
Madrid, 1917

TIMES ALONE
PASSAGEWAYS IN THE HOUSE
AND OTHER POEMS

He andado muchos caminos,
he abierto muchas veredas;
he navegado en cien mares,
y atracado en cien riberas.

En todas partes he visto
caravanas de tristeza,
soberbios y melancólicos
borrachos de sombra negra,

y pedantones al paño
que miran, callan, y piensan
que saben, porque no beben
el vino de las tabernas.

Mala gente que camina
y va apestando la tierra . . .

Y en todas partes he visto
gentes que danzan o juegan,
cuando pueden, y laboran
sus cuatro palmos de tierra.

Nunca, si llegan a un sitio,
preguntan adónde llegan.
Cuando caminan, cabalgan
a lomos de mula vieja,

y no conocen la prisa
ni aun en los días de fiesta.
Donde hay vino, beben vino;
donde no hay vino, agua fresca.

Son buenas gentes que viven,
laboran, pasan y sueñan,
y en un día como tantos,
descansan bajo la tierra.

1

I have walked along many roads,
and opened paths through brush,
I have sailed over a hundred seas
and tied up on a hundred shores.

Everywhere I've gone I've seen
excursions of sadness,
angry and melancholy
drunkards with black shadows,

and academics in offstage clothes
who watch, say nothing, and think
they know, because they do not drink wine
in the ordinary bars.

Evil men who walk around
polluting the earth . . .

And everywhere I've been I've seen
men who dance and play,
when they can, and work
the few inches of ground they have.

If they turn up somewhere,
they never ask where they are.
When they take trips, they ride
on the backs of old mules.

They don't know how to hurry,
not even on holidays.
They drink wine, if there is some,
if not, cool water.

These men are the good ones,
who love, work, walk and dream.
And on a day no different from the rest
they lie down beneath the earth.

RECUERDO INFANTIL

Una tarde parda y fría
de invierno. Los colegiales
estudian. Monotonía
de lluvia tras los cristales.

Es la clase. En un cartel
se representa a Caín
fugitivo, y muerto Abel,
junto a una mancha carmín.

Con timbre sonoro y hueco
truena el maestro, un anciano
mal vestido, enjuto y seco,
que lleva un libro en la mano.

Y todo un coro infantil
va cantando la lección;
"mil veces ciento, cien mil,
mil veces mil, un millón."

Una tarde parda y fría
de invierno. Los colegiales
estudian. Monotonía
de la lluvia en los cristales.

MEMORY FROM CHILDHOOD

A chilly and overcast afternoon
of winter. The students
are studying. Steady boredom
of raindrops across the windowpanes.

Recess over. In a poster
Cain is shown running
away, and Abel dead,
not far from a red spot.

The teacher, with a voice husky and hollow,
is thundering. He is an old man badly dressed,
withered and dried up,
holding a book in his hand.

And the whole children's choir
is singing its lesson:
"one thousand times one hundred is one hundred thousand,
one thousand times one thousand is one million."

A chilly and overcast afternoon
of winter. The students
are studying. Steady boredom
of raindrops across the windowpanes.

La plaza y los naranjos encendidos
con sus frutas redondas y risueñas.

Tumulto de pequeños colegiales
que, al salir en desorden de la escuela,
llenan el aire de la plaza en sombra
con la algazara de sus voces nuevas.

¡Alegría infantil en los rincones
de las ciudades muertas! . . .
¡Y algo nuestro de ayer, que todavía
vemos vagar por estas calles viejas!

3

The square and the brilliant orange trees
with their fruit round and joyful.

Uproar of the young students
piling in confusion out of the school—
they fill the air of the shady square
with the gladness of their fresh voices.

Childlike gaiety in the nooks
of dead cities!
And something we once were, that we still
see walking through these old streets!

4

EN EL ENTIERRO DE UN AMIGO

Tierra le dieron una tarde horrible
del mes de julio, bajo el sol de fuego.

A un paso de la abierta sepultura,
había rosas de podridos pétalos,
entre geranios de áspera fragancia
y roja flor. El cielo
puro y azul. Corría
un aire fuerte y seco.

De los gruesos cordeles suspendido,
pesadamente, descender hicieron
el ataúd al fondo de la fosa
los dos sepultureros ...

Y al reposar sonó con recio golpe,
solemne, en el silencio.

Un golpe de ataúd en tierra es algo
perfectamente serio.

Sobre la negra caja se rompían
los pesados terrones polvorientos ...

El aire se llevaba
de la honda fosa el blanquecino aliento.

—Y tú, sin sombra ya, duerme y reposa,
larga paz a tus huesos ...

Definitivamente,
duerme un sueño tranquilo y verdadero.

THE BURIAL OF A FRIEND

They gave him to earth one horrible afternoon
in July, under a burning sun.

One step from the open hole
roses lay with rotting petals,
geraniums with red flowers
and pungent fragrance. The sky
clear and blue. A strong
and dry wind was blowing.

Two gravediggers
let the coffin hang there
heavily on its fat ropes
and then settle to the bottom . . .

And when it got there it made a loud thump
soberly in the silence.

The sound of a coffin hitting earth
is a sound utterly serious.

Dry lumps of dirt
break on the black box . . .

A whitish breath
rose from the deep hole, and the wind took it.

"And you, with no shadow now, sleep and be;
deep peace to your bones . . .

It is final now,
sleep your untroubled and true dream."

Yo escucho los cantos
de viejas cadencias,
que los niños cantan
cuando en coro juegan,
y vierten en coro
sus almas que sueñan,
cual vierten sus aguas
las fuentes de piedra:
con monotonías
de risas eternas,
que no son alegres,
con lágrimas viejas,
que no son amargas
y dicen tristezas,
tristezas de amores
de antiguas leyendas.

En los labios niños,
las canciones llevan
confusa la historia
y clara la pena;
como clara el agua
lleva su conseja
de viejos amores,
que nunca se cuentan.

Jugando, a la sombra
de una plaza vieja,
los niños cantaban ...

La fuente de piedra
vertía su eterno
cristal de leyenda.

5

I listen to the songs—
in such old meters!—
that the children sing
when they play together.
They pour out in choirs
their dreamy souls
as the stone fountains
pour out their waters:
there is eternal merriment
—a bit monotonous—
not really joyful,
and grief very ancient, ×
not really serious.
They pour out sad things,
sad things about love
and tales from the past.

On the children's lips
as they sing the history
is tangled but
the pain is clear;
so the clear water
tells its garbled tale
of loves long ago
that never get said.

Playing in the shadows
of the ancient square,
the children go on singing . . .

The stone fountain
was pouring out its eternal
fountain of story.

Cantaban los niños
canciones ingenuas,
de un algo que pasa
y que nunca llega:
la historia confusa
y clara la pena.

Seguía su cuento
la fuente serena;
borrada la historia,
contaba la pena.

The children were singing
their innocent songs,
of something which is in motion
yet never arrives:
the history is tangled
but the pain is clear.

The peaceable fountain
continues telling its things;
the history lost,
the pain has found words.

Daba el reloj las doce . . . y eran doce
golpes de azada en tierra . . .
. . . ¡Mi hora! — grité —. . . . El silencio
me respondió: — No temas;
tú no verás caer la última gota
que en la clepsidra tiembla.

Dormirás muchas horas todavía
sobre la orilla vieja,
y encontrarás una mañana pura
amarrada tu barca a otra ribera.

6

The clock struck twelve times . . . and it was a spade
knocked twelve times against the earth.
. . . "It's my turn!" I cried. . . . The silence
answered me: Do not be afraid.
You will never see the last drop fall
that now is trembling in the water clock.

You will still sleep many hours
here on the beach,
and one clear morning you will find
your boat tied to another shore.

Sobre la tierra amarga,
caminos tiene el sueño
laberínticos, sendas tortuosas,
parques en flor y en sombra y en silencio;

criptas hondas, escalas sobre estrellas;
retablos de esperanzas y recuerdos.
Figurillas que pasan y sonríen
— juguetes melancólicos de viejo —;

imágenes amigas,
a la vuelta florida del sendero,
y quimeras rosadas
que hacen camino . . . lejos . . .

7

Dreams have winding
roads going over the embittered
earth, labyrinthine paths,
parks in flower, and in darkness, and in silence;

deep vaults, ladders over the stars;
altarpieces of hopes and memories.
Tiny men who walk past smiling—
melancholy toys of old people . . .

sweet visions
at the flowery turn in the road,
and mythical monsters, rosy ones,
that wander . . . far away . . .

¡Tenue rumor de túnicas que pasan
sobre la infértil tierra! . . .
¡Y lágrimas sonoras
de las campanas viejas!

Las ascuas mortecinas
del horizonte humean . . .
Blancos fantasmas lares
van encendiendo estrellas.

—Abre el balcón. La hora
de una ilusión se acerca . . .
La tarde se ha dormido,
y las campanas sueñan.

8

Faint sound of robes brushing
the exhausted earth!
And so much grief
from the ancient bells!

Dying coals
smoke in the west . . .
Snowy Roman ghosts
go about lighting the stars.

"Open the balcony door. It is time
for the phantasm to come . . .
The afternoon is dozing
and the bells are asleep."

Crece en la plaza en sombra
el musgo, y en la piedra vieja y santa
de la Iglesia. En el atrio hay un mendigo . . .
Más vieja que la iglesia tiene el alma.

Sube muy lento, en las mañanas frías,
por la marmórea grada,
hasta un rincón de piedra . . . Allí aparece
su mano seca entre la rota capa.

Con las órbitas huecas de sus ojos
ha visto cómo pasan
las blancas sombras, en los claros días,
las blancas sombras de las horas santas.

In the shady parts of the square, moss
is growing, and on the sacred old slabs
of the church. A beggar stands on the church porch. . . .
He has a soul older than the church.

On cold mornings he climbs with tremendous slowness
up the marble stairs
toward a stony nook—then the dry hand
appears from his torn cloak.

He has seen, with the dusty sockets
of his eyes,
the white shadows go by, in the sun-filled days,
the white shadows of the holy hours.

Al borde del sendero un día nos sentamos.
Ya nuestra vida es tiempo, y nuestra sola cuita
son las desperantes posturas que tomamos
para aguardar . . . Mas Ella no faltará a la cita.

Close to the road we sit down one day.
Now our life amounts to time, and our sole concern
the attitudes of despair we adopt
while we wait. But She will not fail to arrive.

LA NORIA

La tarde caía
triste y polvorienta.

El agua cantaba
su copla plebeya
en los cangilones
de la noria lenta.

Soñaba la mula,
¡pobre mula vieja!,
al compás de sombra
que en el agua suena.

La tarde caía
triste y polvorienta.

Yo no sé qué noble,
divino poeta,
unió a la amargura
de la eterna rueda

la dulce armonía
del agua que sueña,
y vendó tus ojos,
¡pobre mula vieja! . . .

Mas sé que fué un noble,
divino poeta,
corazón maduro
de sombra y de ciencia.

THE WATER WHEEL

The afternoon arrived
mournful and dusty.

The water was composing
its countrified poem
in the buckets
of the lazy water wheel.

The mule was dreaming—
old and sad mule!
in time to the darkness
that was talking in the water.

The afternoon arrived
mournful and dusty.

I don't know which noble
and religious poet
joined the anguish
of the endless wheel

to the cheerful music
of the dreaming water,
and bandaged your eyes—
old and sad mule! . . .

But it must have been a noble
and religious poet,
a heart made mature
by darkness and art.

GLOSA

Nuestras vidas son los ríos,
que van a dar a la mar,
que es el morir. ¡Gran cantar!

Entre los poetas míos
tiene Manrique un altar.

Dulce goce de vivir:
mala ciencia del pasar,
ciego huir a la mar.

Tras el pavor del morir
está el placer de llegar.

¡Gran placer!
Mas ¿y el horror de volver?
¡Gran pesar!

COMMENTARY

*"Our lives are rivers
and rivers flow and move to the sea,
which is our dying."* Marvellous lines!

Among the poets I admire
I love Manrique the most.

A sweet voluptuousness of living:
tough knowledge of leaving,
blind flight to the sea.

After the fright of dying,
the joy of having arrived.

Great joy!
But—the terror of returning?
Great grief!

Anoche cuando dormía
soñé, ¡ bendita ilusión!,
que una fontana fluía
dentro de mi corazón.
Di, ¿por qué acequia escondida,
agua, vienes hasta mí,
manantial de nueva vida
en donde nunca bebí?

Anoche cuando dormía
soñé, ¡bendita ilusión!,
que una colmena tenía
dentro de mi corazón;
y las doradas abejas
iban fabricando en él,
con las amarguras viejas,
blanca cera y dulce miel.

Anoche cuando dormía
soñé, ¡bendita ilusión!,
que un ardiente sol lucía
dentro de mi corazón.
Era ardiente porque daba
calores de rojo hogar,
y era sol porque alumbraba
y porque hacía llorar.

Anoche cuando dormía
soñé, ¡ bendita ilusión!,
que era Dios lo que tenía
dentro de mi corazón.

Last night, as I was sleeping,
I dreamt—marvellous error!—
that a spring was breaking
out in my heart.
I said: Along which secret aqueduct,
Oh water, are you coming to me,
water of a new life
that I have never drunk?

Last night, as I was sleeping,
I dreamt—marvellous error!—
that I had a beehive
here inside my heart.
And the golden bees
were making white combs
and sweet honey
from my old failures.

Last night, as I was sleeping,
I dreamt—marvellous error!—
that a fiery sun was giving
light inside my heart.
It was fiery because I felt
warmth as from a hearth,
and sun because it gave light
and brought tears to my eyes.

Last night, as I slept,
I dreamt—marvellous error!—
that it was God I had
here inside my heart.

¿Mi corazón se ha dormido?
Colmenares de mis sueños,
¿ya no labráis? ¿Está seca
la noria del pensamiento,
los cangilones vacíos,
girando, de sombra llenos?

No, mi corazón no duerme.
Está despierto, despierto.
Ni duerme ni sueña, mira,
los claros ojos abiertos,
señas lejanas y escucha
a orillas del gran silencio.

Is my soul asleep?
Have those beehives that labor
at night stopped? And the water
wheel of thought,
is it dry, the cups empty,
wheeling, carrying only shadows?

No my soul is not asleep.
It is awake, wide awake.
It neither sleeps nor dreams, but watches,
its clear eyes open,
far-off things, and listens
at the shores of the great silence.

Desgarrada la nube; el arco iris
brillando ya en el cielo,
y en un fanal de lluvia
y sol el campo envuelto.

Desperté. ¿Quién enturbia
los mágicos cristales de mi sueño?
Mi corazón latía
atónito y disperso.

. . . ¡El limonar florido,
el cipresal del huerto,
el prado verde, el sol, el agua, el iris! . . . ,
¡el agua en tus cabellos! . . .

Y todo en la memoria se perdía
como una pompa de jabón al viento.

Clouds ripped open; a rainbow
gleaming now in the sky,
the fields entirely folded inside
the glass bell of rain and sunlight.

I woke up. What is clouding
the magical windowpanes of my dream?
My heart beat
astonished and upset.

The flowering lemon tree,
the cypress in rows in the garden,
the green field, the sun, the water, the rainbow!
drops of water in your hair . . . !

And it all vanished back inside
like a soap bubble in the wind.

Y era el demonio de mi sueño, el ángel
más hermoso. Brillaban
como aceros los ojos victoriosos,
y las sangrientas llamas
de su antorcha alumbraron
la honda cripta del alma.

—¿Vendrás conmigo?—. No, jamás; las tumbas
y los muertos me espantan.
Pero la férrea mano
mi diestra atenazaba.

—Vendrás conmigo . . . Y avancé en mi sueño
cegado por la roja luminaria.
Y en la cripta sentí sonar cadenas,
y rebullir de fieras enjauladas.

And he was the demon of my dreams, the most handsome
of all angels. His victorious eyes
blazed like steel,
and the flames that fell
from his torch like drops
lit up the deep dungeon of the soul.

"Will you go with me?" "No, never! Tombs
and dead bodies frighten me."
But his iron hand
took mine.

"You will go with me." . . . And in my dream I walked
blinded by his red torch.
In the dungeon I heard the sound of chains
and the stirrings of beasts that were in cages.

Desde el umbral de un sueño me llamaron . . .
Era la buena voz, la voz querida.

—Dime: ¿vendrás conmigo a ver el alma? . . .
Llegó a mi corazón una caricia.

—Contigo siempre . . . Y avancé en mi sueño
por una larga, escueta galería,
sintiendo el roce de la veste pura
y el palpitar suave de la mano amiga.

From the door sill of a dream they called my name. . . .
It was the good voice, the voice I loved so much.

"—Listen: will you go with me to visit the soul? . . ."
A soft stroke reached up to my heart.

"With you always" . . . And in my dream I walked
down a long and solitary corridor,
aware of the touching of the pure robe,
and the soft beating of blood in the hand that loved me.

Si yo fuera un poeta
galante, cantaría
a vuestros ojos un cantar tan puro
como en el mármol blanco el agua limpia.

Y en una estrofa de agua
todo el cantar sería:

«Ya sé que no responden a mis ojos,
que ven y no preguntan cuando miran,
los vuestros claros, vuestros ojos tienen
la buena luz tranquila,
la buena luz del mundo en flor, que he visto
desde los brazos de mi madre un día.»

If I were a poet
of love, I would make
a poem for your eyes as clear
as the transparent water in the marble pool.

And in my water poem
this is what I would say:

"I know your eyes do not answer mine,
they look and do not question when they look:
your clear eyes, your eyes have
the calm and good light,
the good light of the blossoming world, that I saw
one day from the arms of my mother."

Y nada importa ya que el vino de oro
rebose de tu copa cristalina,
o el agrio zumo enturbie el puro vaso . . .

Tú sabes las secretas galerías
del alma, los caminos de los sueños,
y la tarde tranquila
donde van a morir . . . Allí te aguardan

las hadas silenciosas de la vida,
y hacia un jardín de eterna primavera
te llevarán un día.

It doesn't matter now if the golden wine
floats abundantly in your crystal cup,
or if the bitter juice clouds the pure glass. . . .

You know the secret passageways
of the soul, the roads that dreams take,
and the calm evening
where they go to die. . . . There the good and silent spirits

of life are waiting for you,
and one day they will carry you
to a garden of eternal spring.

Llamó a mi corazón, un claro día,
con un perfume de jazmín, el viento.

—A cambio de este aroma,
todo el aroma de tus rosas quiero.
—No tengo rosas; flores
en mi jardín no hay ya: todas han muerto.

Me llevaré los llantos de las fuentes,
las hojas amarillas y los mustios pétalos.
Y el viento huyó . . . Mi corazón sangraba . . .
Alma, ¿qué has hecho de tu pobre huerto?

The wind, one brilliant day, called
to my soul with an aroma of jasmine.

"In return for this jasmine odor,
I'd like all the odor of your roses."

"I have no roses; I have no flowers left now
in my garden. . . . All are dead."

"Then I'll take the waters of the fountains,
and the yellow leaves and the dried-up petals."

The wind left. . . . I wept. I said to my soul,
"What have you done with the garden entrusted to you?"

La casa tan querida
donde habitaba ella,
sobre un montón de escombros arruinada
o derruída, enseña
el negro y carcomido
maltrabado esqueleto de madera.

La luna está vertiendo
su clara luz en sueños que platea
en las ventanas. Mal vestido y triste,
voy caminando por la calle vieja.

The house I loved so much
—she lived there—
rising above a great mound of bricks and chunks,
broken down
and collapsed, shows now
its black and worm-eaten
badly lasting skeleton of wood.

The moon is pouring down
her clear light in dreams that turn
the windows silver. Poorly dressed and sad,
I go walking along the old street.

Yo, como Anacreonte,
quiero cantar, reír y echar al viento
las sabias amarguras
y los graves consejos,

y quiero, sobre todo, emborracharme,
ya lo sabéis . . . ¡Grotesco!
Pura fe en el morir, pobre alegría
y macabro danzar antes de tiempo.

Like Anacreon,
I want to sing, and to laugh, and to throw
to the wind
the sophisticated sarcasms, and the sobering proverbs.

And I want even more to get drunk—
you know about it—bizarre!
A true faith in dying, a thin joy,
strange dancing a little ahead of time.

¡Oh tarde luminosa!
El aire está encantado.
La blanca cigüeña
dormita volando,
y las golondrinas se cruzan, tendidas
las alas agudas al viento dorado,
y en la tarde risueña se alejan
volando, soñando . . .

Y hay una que torna como la saeta,
las alas agudas tendidas al aire sombrío.
buscando su negro rincón del tejado.

La blanca cigüeña,
como un garabato,
tranquila y disforme, ¡tan disparatada!,
sobre el campanario.

Oh, evening full of light!
The air hovers enchanted.
The white stork half
sleeps as he flies,
and the swallows cross and recross, the pointed wings
stretched out in the golden wind,
and in the glad evening wheel far off
flying dreaming. . . .

And one turns back like an arrow,
his pointed wings stretched out in the darkening wind,
finding his black hole in the roof tiles!

And the white stork,
shaped like an iron hook,
serene and deformed—so absurd!—
on the bell tower!

Es una tarde cenicienta y mustia,
destartalada, como el alma mía;
y es esta vieja angustia
que habita mi usual hipocondría.
    La causa de esta angustia no consigo
ni vagamente comprender siquiera;
pero recuerdo y, recordando, digo:
—Sí, yo era niño, y tú, mi compañera.

*

    Y no es verdad, dolor, yo te conozco,
tú eres nostalgia de la vida buena
y soledad de corazón sombrío,
de barco sin naufragio y sin estrella.
    Como perro olvidado que no tiene
huella ni olfato y yerra
por los caminos, sin camino, como
el niño que en la noche de una fiesta
    se pierde entre el gentío
y el aire polvoriento y las candelas
chispeantes, atónito, y asombra
su corazón de música y de pena,
    así voy yo, borracho melancólico,
guitarrista lunático, poeta,
y pobre hombre en sueños,
siempre buscando a Dios entre la niebla.

The evening is greyish and gloomy,
shabby, and my spirit is the same.
The anxiety I have is the one I know,
neighbor to my old hypochondria.

I don't know what causes this anxiety;
I don't even have a general understanding;
but I think back, and, remembering, I say:
"Yes I was a boy, and you were my only friend."

*

Sorrow, it is not true that I know you;
you are the nostalgia for a good life,
and the aloneness of the soul in shadow,
the sailing ship without wreck and without guide.

Like an abandoned dog who cannot find
a smell or a track and roams
along the roads, with no road, like
the child who in a night of the fair

gets lost among the crowd,
and the air is dusty, and the candles
fluttering,—astounded, his heart
weighed down by music and by pain;

that's how I am, drunk, sad by nature,
a mad and lunar guitarist, a poet,
and an ordinary man lost in dreams,
searching constantly for God among the mists.

CAMPO

La tarde está muriendo
como un hogar humilde que se apaga.

Allá, sobre los montes,
quedan algunas brasas.

Y ese árbol roto en el camino blanco
hace llorar de lástima.

¡Dos ramas en el tronco herido, y una
hoja marchita y negra en cada rama!

¿Lloras? . . . Entre los álamos de oro,
lejos, la sombra del amor te aguarda.

FIELD

The afternoon is dying
like a simple houschold fire that goes out.

There, above the mountains,
a few coals are left.

And that tree on the white road, broken,
makes you cry with compassion.

Two branches on the torn trunk, and one
leaf, withered and black, on each branch!

Are you crying now? . . . In the golden poplars
far off, the shadow of love is waiting for you.

RENACIMIENTO

Galerías del alma . . . ¡El alma niña!
Su clara luz risueña;
y la pequeña historia,
y la alegría de la vida nueva . . .

¡Ah, volver a nacer, y andar camino,
ya recobrada la perdida senda!

Y volver a sentir en nuestra mano,
aquel latido de la mano buena
de nuestra madre . . . Y caminar en sueños
por amor de la mano que nos lleva.

*

En nuestras almas todo
por misteriosa mano se gobierna.
Incomprensibles, mudas,
nada sabemos de las almas nuestras.

Las más hondas palabras
del sabio nos enseñan,
lo que el silbar del viento cuando sopla,
o el sonar de las aguas cuando ruedan.

REBIRTH

Passageways of the soul! The soul like a young woman!
Her clear smiling light
and the history not long,
and the joy of a new life . . .

Yes, to be born again, and walk the road,
having found the lost path!

To feel in our hand once more
the pulse in the good hand
of our mother . . . And to walk through life in dreams
out of love for the hand that guides us.

*

In our souls everything
moves guided by a mysterious hand.
We know nothing of our own souls
that are ununderstandable and say nothing.

The deepest words
of the wise man teach us
the same as the whistle of the wind when it blows
or the sound of the water when it is flowing.

Tal vez la mano, en sueños,
del sembrador de estrellas,
hizo sonar la música olvidada

como una nota de la lira inmensa,
y la ola humilde a nuestros labios vino
de unas pocas palabras verdaderas.

It's possible that while sleeping the hand
that sows the seeds of stars
started the ancient music going again

—like a note from a great harp—
and the frail wave came to our lips
as one or two honest words.

Y podrás conocerte recordando
del pasado soñar los turbios lienzos,
en este día triste en que caminas
con los ojos abiertos.

De toda la memoria, sólo vale
el don preclaro de evocar los sueños.

You can know yourself, if you bring up
those cloudy canvases from your dreams,
today, this day, when you walk
awake, open-eyed.

Memory is valuable for one thing,
astonishing: it brings dreams back.

FROM

THE COUNTRYSIDE
OF CASTILE

〜〜〜〜〜〜〜〜〜〜〜〜〜〜〜〜〜〜〜〜〜〜〜〜〜〜

CAMPOS DE CASTILLA

FIRST EDITION 1912

ENLARGED IN 1917

"ONLY IN lazy moments does a poet concentrate on interpreting his dreams, and picking things out of them he can use in his poems. Dream study has not yet produced anything of importance in poetry. The poems written while we are awake, even those less successful, are more original and more beautiful, and sometimes more wild than those made from our dreams. I can say this because I spent many years of my life thinking just the opposite. But a part of wisdom is changing one's opinions."

Machado wants the conscious mind to take part, even more vigorously than it did in *Soledades*, while the poem itself remains mysterious and committed to depth. This idea marks a big shift from the aims of *Soledades*. During the five years that he spent in Soria, from 1907 to 1912, he wrote *The Countryside of Castile (Campos de Castilla)*, first version, and I'll mention five areas in which I've noticed shifts, turns, changes, increases in depth. He responds, in this book, to his mother's question: "What have you done with your eyes?"

Living in Soria, he tries to see the countryside and to describe what a dawn in Castile is like, rather than to remain content with a dreamy or poetic version of dawn. He understands that being spiritually awake and keeping the eyes open are connected. "One has to keep the eyes well open in order to see things as they are, and still more open to see them as other than they are, and open them still more widely in order to see things as better than they are."

One also senses that he experienced something entirely new in his love for Leonor. We could say that Machado, with his marvellous introversion, had met years before his feminine self, or feminine soul, far inside himself, at the end of some

passageway in a dream. He experienced that acquaintance-
ship; knew "her." But when he met Leonor he experienced
that feminine soul in another person. Isn't a man's feminine
soul younger than he is? The soul that was once inside him,
or only inside him, is now outside as well, and what once
tended to separate him from others now draws him close to
one human being, bonds him. His faith in the surprises of
the universe deepens.

Third, he continues to search in his work for "the things of
feeling that all men possess." He moves to bring the private
close to the public, or, more exactly, to embody his private
introverted perceptions in poetic forms so available they could
be called public, for even the people in Spain that can neither
read nor write know the coplas (the popular songs) and ballads.
He compared the coplas to a common earthen jug that he
once saw lying beside a spring which people could drink from.
In this deepening he resembles Yeats, who, shortly before he
died, referring to a recent article, said that the greatest honor
anyone could pay him was to use the word "public" about
his language.

In accordance perhaps with his determination to write with
eyes open, he takes a step few twentieth-century poets have
taken: he asks thinking to enter his poems. He is not afraid
that thinking will evict feeling, and it doesn't; and he recog-
nizes it as a power, a life energy. Thinking often shows itself
in the willingness to break the hoped-for unity. Yeats says:

> The intellect of man is forced to choose
> Perfection of the life or of the work.

Machado says:

> There are two sorts of consciousness:
> one involves light, one patience.

He opposes the church because it depresses thinking:

> Make noise, anvils; be silent, you church bells!

He brings the widest possible poles into a small poem. For
example: Does everything pass away? Or is what passes away

only a veil, and behind that is there something that lasts forever?

> *All things die, and all things live forever;*
> *but our task is to die,*
> *to die while making roads,*
> *roads over the sea.*

His thinking is sprightly, and he takes risks with it.

Finally, one senses in *The Countryside of Castile* that he has passed through some intense burning, some testing, a cooking of some kind, which has changed some of his slow lead into gold. He no longer has a bushel-basket over his candle, but allows his light to radiate, and is very clear about what sort of light it is.

> *I never wanted fame,*
> *nor wanted to leave my poems*
> *behind in the memory of men.*
> *I love the subtle worlds,*
> *delicate, almost without weight*
> *like soap bubbles.*
> *I enjoy seeing them take the color*
> *of sunlight and scarlet, float*
> *in the blue sky, then*
> *suddenly quiver and break.*

Here are the words he wrote about *The Countryside of Castile*:

In a third collection I published my second book, *Campos de Castilla* (1912). Five years in and around Soria, which is now sacred to me — there I married and there I lost my wife, whom I adored — drew me, my vision and my feelings, into what was deeply Castilian. Moreover, my set of ideas had changed very much. We are victims, I thought, of a double hallucination. If we look outward, and concentrate on entering things, our external world begins to lose solidity, and if we conclude that it exists not in and for itself, but exists because of us, it ends by dissolving. However, if, moved by our private reality, we turn our eyes inward, then the world pushes in on us, and it is our interior world, our being, that disappears. What to do then? Weave the thread given to us, dream our dream and live; it is the only way we can achieve the miracle of growth. A man attentive to himself and trying to overhear himself drowns the only voice he could hear — his own; but other voices confuse him. Are we then doomed to be merely observers? But when we see, reason is present, and reason analyzes and dissolves. The reason will soon bring the whole theater down, and finally, our shadow alone will be projected against the background. As for the poet, I thought that his job was to create new poems out of what is eternally human, spirited stories that have their own life, even though they came from him. I considered the old narrative *romance* the supreme expression of poetry, and I wanted to write a new book of them. *La tierra de Alvergonzàlez* came from this longing. The last thing I want is to resuscitate the genre in its traditional sense. Working up of old-style ballads—chivalrous or moorish—was never to my taste, and all imitations of archaic things seem ridiculous to me. It's true that I learned to read in the *Romancero general* which my uncle Augustín Durán collected; but my own narratives did not spring from heroic tales, but rather from the people who composed them and the parts of the country where they were sung; my narratives look to what is fundamentally human, to the Castilian countryside and to the first book of Moses, which is called *Génesis.*

You will come on many poems in this book a long way from the propositions I have just mentioned. Many of the poems spring from a preoccupation with the nation; others from a simple love of nature that in me is far stronger than the love of art. Finally, some of the poems show the many hours of my life spent—some would say wasted—thinking about the puzzles of the human being and the outer world.

Antonio Machado
Madrid, 1917

THE COUNTRYSIDE

OF CASTILE

RETRATO

Mi infancia son recuerdos de un patio de Sevilla,
y un huerto claro donde madura el limonero;
mi juventud, veinte años en tierra de Castilla;
mi historia, algunos casos que recordar no quiero.

Ni un seductor Mañara, ni un Bradomín he sido
—ya conocéis mi torpe aliño indumentario—,
mas recibí la flecha que me asignó Cupido,
y amé cuanto ellas puedan tener de hospitalario.

Hay en mis venas gotas de sangre jacobina,
pero mi verso brota de manantial sereno;
y, más que un hombre al uso que sabe su doctrina,
soy, en el buen sentido de la palabra, bueno.

Adoro la hermosura, y en la moderna estética
corté las viejas rosas del huerto de Ronsard;
mas no amo los afeites de la actual cosmética,
ni soy un ave de esas del nuevo gay-trinar.

Desdeño las romanzas de los tenores huecos
y el coro de los grillos que cantan a la luna.
A distinguir me paro las voces de los ecos,
y escucho solamente, entre las voces, una.

¿Soy clásico o romántico? No sé. Dejar quisiera
mi verso, como deja el capitán su espada:
famosa por la mano viril que la blandiera,
no por el docto oficio del forjador preciada.

Converso con el hombre que siempre va conmigo
—quien habla solo espera hablar a Dios un día—;
mi soliloquio es plática con este buen amigo
que me enseñó el secreto de la filantropía.

PORTRAIT

My childhood is memories of a patio in Seville,
and a garden where sunlit lemons are growing yellow;
my youth twenty years on the earth of Castile;
what I lived a few things you'll forgive me for omitting.

A great seducer I was not, nor the lover of Juliet;
—the oafish way I dress is enough to say that—
but the arrow Cupid planned for me I got,
and I loved whenever women found a home in me.

A flow of leftist blood moves through my body,
but my poems rise from a calm and deep spring.
There is a man of rule who behaves as he should, but more
than him, I am, in the good sense of the word, good.

I adore beauty, and following contemporary thought
have cut some old roses from the garden of Ronsard;
but the new lotions and feathers are not for me;
I am not one of the blue jays who sing so well.

I dislike hollow tenors who warble of love,
and the chorus of crickets singing to the moon.
I fall silent so as to separate voices from echoes,
and I listen among the voices to one voice and only one.

Am I classic or Romantic? Who knows. I want to leave
my poetry as a fighter leaves his sword, known
for the masculine hand that closed around it,
not for the coded mark of the proud forger.

I talk always to the man who walks along with me;
—men who talk to themselves hope to talk to God someday—
My soliloquies amount to discussions with this friend,
who taught me the secret of loving human beings.

Y al cabo, nada os debo; debéisme cuanto he escrito
A mi trabajo acudo, con mi dinero pago
el traje que me cubre y la mansión que habito,
el pan que me alimenta y el lecho en donde yago.

Y cuando llegue el día del último viaje,
y esté al partir la nave que nunca ha de tornar,
me encontraréis a bordo ligero de equipaje,
casi desnudo, como los hijos de la mar.

In the end, I owe you nothing; you owe me what I've written.
I turn to my work; with what I've earned I pay
for my clothes and hat, the house in which I live,
the food that feeds my body, the bed on which I sleep.

And when the day arrives for the last leaving of all,
and the ship that never returns to port is ready to go,
you'll find me on board, light, with few belongings,
almost naked like the children of the sea.

¿ERES TÚ, GUADARRAMA

¿Eres tú, Guadarrama, viejo amigo,
la sierra gris y blanca,
la sierra de mis tardes madrileñas
que yo veía en el azul pintada?

Por tus barrancos hondos
y por tus cumbres agrias,
mil Guadarramas y mil soles vienen,
cabalgando conmigo, a tus entrañas.

Camino de Balsaín, 1911

OH, GUADARRAMA RANGE

Oh, Guadarrama range, is it you, old friend,
that smoky bluish range,
long Madrid afternoons when I used to see
your peaks painted against the blue sky?

As I ride up your deep valleys,
and ride past your sharp-honed ridges,
a thousand suns and a thousand Guadarramas
ride with me, as I go far, deep into you.

On the Balsain road, 1911

AMANECER DE OTOÑO

A Julio Romero de Torres

Una larga carretera
entre grises peñascales,
y alguna humilde pradera
donde pacen negros toros. Zarzas, malezas, jarales.

Está la tierra mojada
por las gotas del rocío,
y la alameda dorada,
hacia la curva del río.

Tras los montes de violeta
quebrado el primer albor;
a la espalda la escopeta,
entre sus galgos agudos, caminando un cazador.

FALL DAWN
For Julio Romero de Torres

The road runs along
between grayish rock spines,
and a few grassy spots, pastures,
black bulls eating. Blackberries, weeds, wild roses.

Earth still carries moisture
from the night dew,
and the poplars have yellowed
along the river's curve.

The first light of dawn
lifts from the violet peaks;
a hunter walks, with his gun
shouldered, on the road between his tense dogs.

CAMPOS DE SORIA

1

Es la tierra de Soria árida y fría.
Por las colinas y las sierras calvas,
verdes pradillos, cerros cenicientos,
la primavera pasa
dejando entre las hierbas olorosas
sus diminutas margaritas blancas.
La tierra no revive, el campo sueña.
Al empezar abril está nevada
la espalda del Moncayo;
el caminante lleva en su bufanda
envueltos cuello y boca, y los pastores
pasan cubiertos con sus luengas capas.

TWO POEMS FROM
"THE COUNTRYSIDE OF SORIA"

1

The ground around Soria is washed out and cold.
Through the ridges and the bald peaks,
the miniature green meadows, the ash-colored hills,
spring travels
leaving white margarita blossoms behind
among the wild-smelling grasses.

The earth does not awake, the country sleeps on.
Moncayo's spine carries snow
in early April;
Those walking wear scarves
protecting throat and mouth, and the shepherds
go past hidden in their trailing capes.

¡Soria fría. *Soria pura,*
cabeza de Extremadura,
con su castillo guerrero
arruinado, sobre el Duero;
con sus murallas roídas
y sus casas denegridas!

¡Muerta ciudad de señores
soldados o cazadores;
de portales con escudos
de cien linajes hidalgos,
y de famélicos galgos,
de galgos flacos y agudos,
que pululan
por las sórdidas callejas,
y a la medianoche ululan,
cuando graznan las cornejas!

¡Soria fría! La campana
de la Audiencia da la una.
Soria, ciudad castellana
¡tan bella! bajo la luna.

Cold Soria, intense Soria,
head of Estremadura,
your military castle
by the Duero thrown down,
your walls eaten away,
and houses turning black!

Dead city of knights,
harquebusiers or hunters;
elaborate door frames
identifying lineages,
tense and lean greyhounds,
starving greyhounds as well
who breed abundantly
in the filthy alleys
and howl at midnight
when the crows caw!

Cold Soria! The bells
on the courthouse announce one.
Soria, Castilian city—
so beautiful!—under the moon.

CAMINOS

De la ciudad moruna
tras las murallas viejas,
yo contemplo la tarde silenciosa,
a solas con mi sombra y con mi pena.

El río va corriendo,
entre sombrías huertas
y grises olivares,
por los alegres campos de Baeza.

Tienen las vides pámpanos dorados
sobre las rojas cepas.
Guadalquivir, como un alfanje roto
y disperso, reluce y espeja.

Lejos, los montes duermen
envueltos en la niebla,
niebla de otoño, maternal; descansan
la rudas moles de su ser de piedra
en esta tibia tarde de noviembre,
tarde piadosa, cárdena y violeta.

El viento ha sacudido
los mustios olmos de la carretera,
levantando en rosados torbellinos
el polvo de la tierra.
La luna está subiendo
amoratada, jadeante y llena.

Los caminitos blancos
se cruzan y se alejan,
buscando los dispersos caseríos
del valle y de la sierra.
Caminos de los campos . . .
¡Ay, ya no puedo caminar con ella!

COUNTRY ROADS

From this Moorish city,
behind its medieval ramparts,
I watch the sun quietly setting
alone with my shadow and my pain.

The Guadalquiver
between shadow-filled orchards
and grey olive groves
penetrates the carefree fields of Baeza.

Grapevines show gold
above their red trunks.
The river, like a sword broken and tossed
in pieces, bits of a mirror, shines.

Far away, the peaks of Castile sleep
inside the grey fog, the maternal
fog of November; stony humps
rest from their job of being stone
in this warm evening
which is violet, mauve, and forgiving.

Wind has torn some leaves
off the withered elms along the road,
and it lifts rosy
whirlwinds of dust. . . .
The moon rises,
purple, deep-chested, and full.

The white cart paths
cross each other and wander off
looking for farmhouses
in the foothills and low places.
Roads through the fields—
that I can no longer take with her!

SEÑOR, YA ME ARRANCASTE

Señor, ya me arrancaste lo que yo más quería.
Oye otra vez, Dios mío, mi corazón clamar.
Tu voluntad se hizo, Señor, contra la mía.
Señor, ya estamos solos mi corazón y el mar.

LORD, YOU HAVE RIPPED AWAY

Lord, you have ripped away from me what I loved most.
One more time, O God, hear me cry out inside.
"Your will be done," it was done, and mine not.
My heart and the sea are together, Lord, and alone.

DICE LA ESPERANZA

Dice la esperanza: un día
la verás, si bien esperas.
Dice la desesperanza:
sólo tu amargura es ella.
Late, corazón . . . No todo
se lo ha tragado la tierra.

HOPE SAYS

Hope says: Someday you will
see her, if you know how to wait.
Despair says:
She is only your bitterness now.
Beat, heart . . . The earth
has not swallowed everything.

ALLÁ, EN LAS TIERRAS ALTAS

Allá, en las tierras altas,
por donde traza el Duero
su curva de ballesta
en torno a Soria, entre plomizos cerros
y manchas de raídos encinares,
mi corazón está vagando, en sueños...

¿No ves, Leonor, los álamos del río
con sus ramajes yertos?
Mira el Moncayo azul y blanco; dame
tu mano y paseemos.
Por estos campos de la tierra mía,
bordados de olivares polvorientos,
voy caminando solo,
triste, cansado, pensativo y viejo.

There, in that high plateau,
where the Duero River draws back
its crossbow
around Soria, among lead-colored hills,
and patches of worn-out oaks,
my heart is walking about, daydreaming. . . .

Leonor, do you see the river poplars
with their still branches?
You can see Moncayo, bluish and white; give me
your hand, and we will walk.
Through these fields of my country,
with their embroidery of dusty olives,
I go walking alone,
sad, tired, thoughtful and old.

SOÑÉ QUE TÚ ME LLEVABAS

Soñé que tú me llevabas
por una blanca vereda,
en medio del campo verde,
hacia el azul de las sierras,
hacia los montes azules,
una mañana serena.

Sentí tu mano en la mía,
tu mano de compañera,
tu voz de niña en mi oído
como una campana nueva,
como una campana virgen
de un alba de primavera.
¡Eran tu voz y tu mano,
en sueños, tan verdaderas! . . .
Vive, esperanza, ¡quién sabe
lo que se traga la tierra!

I DREAMT

I dreamt you guided me
down a white path
leading through green fields,
toward the blue of the mountains,
toward the blue mountains;
the morning air was clear.

I felt your hand in mine,
your truly friendly hand,
your girlish voice in my ear
like a bell never used,
like a bell never touched,
ringing in early spring dawn.
It was your voice, your hand,
as I dreamt, so true and exact!
Well, hope, live on . . . Is it certain
how much the earth actually eats?

UNA NOCHE DE VERANO

Una noche de verano
— estaba abierto el balcón
y la puerta de mi casa —
la muerte en mi casa entró.
Se fué acercando a su lecho
— ni siquiera me miró —,
con unos dedos muy finos,
algo muy tenue rompió.
Silenciosa y sin mirarme,
la muerte otra vez pasó
delante de mí. ¿Qué has hecho?
La muerte no respondió.
Mi niña quedó tranquila,
dolido mi corazón.
¡Ay, lo que la muerte ha roto
era un hilo entre los dos!

ONE SUMMER NIGHT

One summer night—
my balcony door stood open
and the front door also—
death entered my house.
He approached her bed—
not even noticing me—
and with very fine hands
broke something delicate.
Death crossed the room
a second time. What did you do?
He did not answer.
I saw no change in her,
but my heart felt heavy.
I knew what he broke:
It was the thread between us!

PROVERBIOS Y CANTARES

1

Nunca perseguí gloria
ni dejar en la memoria
de los hombres mi canción;
yo amo los mundos sutiles,
ingrávidos y gentiles
como pompas de jabón.
Me gusta verlos pintarse
de sol y grana, volar
bajo el cielo azul, temblar
súbitamente y quebrarse.

2

¿Para qué llamar caminos
a los surcos del azar? . . .
Todo el que camina anda,
como Jesús, sobre el mar.

3

Cantad conmigo en coro: Saber, nada sabemos,
de arcano mar vinimos, a ignota mar iremos . . .
Y entre los dos misterios está el enigma grave;
tres arcas cierra una desconocida llave.
La luz nada ilumina y el sabio nada enseña.
¿Qué dice la palabra? ¿Qué el agua de la peña?

FOURTEEN POEMS CHOSEN FROM "MORAL PROVERBS AND FOLK SONGS"

1

I never wanted fame,
nor wanted to leave my poems
behind in the memory of men.
I love the subtle worlds,
delicate, almost without weight
like soap bubbles.
I enjoy seeing them take the color
of sunlight and scarlet, float
in the blue sky, then
suddenly quiver and break.

2

Why should we call
these accidental furrows roads?
Everyone who moves on walks
like Jesus, on the sea.

3

Let us sing together: know? We know nothing.
We come from a hidden ocean, and go to an unknown ocean.
And between those two mysteries there is a third serious
      puzzle;
one key we know nothing of locks three chests.
The light illuminates nothing, and the wise man teaches
      nothing.
What does human language say? What does the water in the
      rock say?

4

¡Ah, cuando yo era niño
soñaba con los héroes de la Ilíada!
Áyax era más fuerte que Diomedes,
Héctor, más fuerte que Áyax,
y Aquiles el más fuerte; porque era
el más fuerte . . . ¡Inocencias de la infancia!
¡Ah, cuando yo era niño
soñaba con los héroes de la Ilíada!

5

Poned sobre los campos
un carbonero, un sabio y un poeta.
Veréis cómo el poeta admira y calla,
el sabio mira y piensa . . .
Seguramente, el carbonero busca
las moras o las setas.
Llevadlos al teatro
y sólo el carbonero no bosteza.
Quien prefiere lo vivo a lo pintado
es el hombre que piensa, canta o sueña.
El carbonero tiene
llena de fantasías la cabeza.

6

Yo amo a Jesús, que nos dijo:
Cielo y tierra pasarán.
Cuando cielo y tierra pasen
mi palabra quedará.
¿Cuál fué, Jesús, tu palabra?
¿Amor? ¿Perdón? ¿Caridad?
Todas tus palabras fueron
una palabra: Velad.

4

Oh, I daydreamed as a boy
about the heroes of the *Iliad*!
Ajax was stronger than Diomedes,
Hector stronger than Ajax,
and Achilles strongest of all; because
he was the strongest! . . . Innocent ideas of boyhood!
Yes, I daydreamed as a boy
about the heroes of the *Iliad*!

5

Put out on the fields
a physical laborer, a thinker, and a poet.
You will see how the poet is enthusiastic
and silent, the thinker looks and thinks. . . .
The laborer looks around, probably,
for blackberries and mushrooms.
Take them to the theatre,
and only the laborer isn't bored.
The one who prefers what is alive
over what is made up
is the person who writes, dreams, or sings.
The head of the physical laborer
is full of fantasies.

6

I love Jesus, who said to us:
Heaven and earth will pass away.
When heaven and earth have passed away,
my word will remain.
What was your word, Jesus?
Love? Affection? Forgiveness?
All your words were
one word: Wakeup.

7

Hay dos modos de conciencia:
una es luz, y otra, paciencia.
Una estriba en alumbrar
un poquito el hondo mar;
otra, en hacer penitencia
con caña o red, y esperar
el pez, como pescador.
Dime tú: ¿Cuál es mejor?
¿Conciencia de visionario
que mira en el hondo acuario
peces vivos,
fugitivos,
que no se pueden pescar,
o esa maldita faena
de ir arrojando a la arena,
muertos, las peces del mar?

8

Bueno es saber que los vasos
nos sirven para beber;
lo malo es que no sabemos
para qué sirve la sed.

9

¿Dices que nada se crea?
No te importe, con el barro
de la tierra, haz una copa
para que beba tu hermano.

10

¿Dices que nada se crea?
Alfarero, a tus cacharros.
Haz tu copa y no te importe
si no puedes hacer barro.

7

There are two sorts of consciousness:
one involves light, one patience.
One has to do with piercing
the ocean a little with light;
the other has more guilt—
with a net or pole, one waits
like a fisherman, for fish.
Tell me: Which is better?
Religious consciousness
that sees in the deep ocean
fish alive,
going their way,
that will never be caught?
Or this job I have, boring,
picking fish from the net
and throwing them on the sand, dead?

8

It is good knowing that glasses
are to drink from;
the bad thing is not to know
what thirst is for.

9

You say nothing is created new?
Don't worry about it, with the mud
of the earth, make a cup
from which your brother can drink.

10

You say nothing is created new?
Potter, go to your shed.
Make your cup, and don't worry
if you aren't able to make clay.

11

Todo pasa y todo queda,
pero lo nuestro es pasar,
pasar haciendo caminos,
caminos sobre la mar.

12

Morir . . . ¿Caer como gota
de mar en el mar inmenso?
¿O ser lo que nunca he sido:
uno, sin sombra y sin sueño,
un solitario que avanza
sin camino y sin espejo?

13

Cuatro cosas tiene el hombre
que no sirven en la mar:
ancla, gobernalle y remos,
y miedo de naufragar.

14

Ya hay un español que quiere
vivir y a vivir empieza,
entre una España que muere
y otra España que bosteza.
Españolito que vienes
al mundo, te guarde Dios.
Una de las dos Españas
ha de helarte el corazón.

11

All things die and all things live forever;
but our task is to die,
to die making roads,
roads over the sea.

12

To die . . . To fall like a drop
of water into the big ocean?
Or to be what I've never been:
a man without a shadow, without a dream,
a man all alone walking,
without a mirror, and with no road?

13

Mankind owns four things
that are no good at sea:
rudder, anchor, oars,
and the fear of going down.

14

There is a Spaniard today, who wants
to live and is starting to live,
between one Spain dying
and another Spain yawning.
Little Spaniard just now coming
into the world, may God keep you.
One of those two Spains
will freeze your heart.

A DON FRANCISCO GINER DE LOS RÍOS

Como se fué el maestro,
la luz de esta mañana
me dijo: Van tres días
que mi hermano Francisco no trabaja.
¿Murió? . . . Sólo sabemos
que se nos fué por una senda clara,
diciéndonos: Hacedme
un duelo de labores y esperanzas.
Sed buenos y no más, sed lo que he sido
entre vosotros: alma.
Vivid, la vida sigue,
los muertos mueren y las sombras pasan;
lleva quien deja y vive el que ha vivido.
¡Yunques, sonad; enmudeced, campanas!

Y hacia otra luz más pura
partió el hermano de la luz del alba,
del sol de los talleres,
el viejo alegre de la vida santa.
. . . ¡Oh, si, llevad, amigos,
su cuerpo a la montaña,
a los azules montes
del ancho Guadarrama.
Allí hay barrancos hondos
de pinos verdes donde el viento canta.
Su corazón repose
bajo una encina casta,
en tierra de tomillos, donde juegan
mariposas doradas . . .
Allí el maestro un día
soñaba un nuevo florecer de España.

Baeza, 21 febrero 1915

FOR DON FRANCISCO
GINER DE LOS RÍOS

At the time the master disappeared,
the morning light
said to me: "For three days
my brother Francisco has not worked.
Has he died?" . . . All we know
is that he has gone off on a clear road,
telling us this: Show
your grief for me in work and hope.
Be good, forget the rest, be
what I have been among you: a soul.
Live, life goes on,
the dead go on dying, the shadows go by,
the man who abandons still has, and the man who has lived
    is alive.
Make noise, anvils; be silent, you church bells!

So the brother of the morning light,
the old happy man with a holy life,
leaving the sun of his work,
went off toward a purer light.
. . . Oh yes, my friends, carry
his body to the mountain!
to the blue hills
of the Guadarrama!
There I know deep ravines
with green pines where the wind sings.
His heart can rest
under an ordinary oak
in the thyme fields, where the golden
butterflies are fluttering. . . .
One day the master there
imagined a new blossoming of Spain.

Baeza, February 21, 1915

(Francisco Giner de los Ríos was the founder of the Free Institution of Learning in Madrid, where so many writers went. During Machado's lifetime he led most of the efforts toward reform of education.)

FROM

NEW POEMS

(NUEVAS CANCIONES)

1930

⟨∼⟩∼⟨∼⟩∼⟨∼⟩∼⟨∼⟩∼⟨∼⟩∼⟨∼⟩∼⟨∼⟩∼⟨∼⟩∼⟨∼⟩

THE COLLECTED WORKS OF A
POET WHO NEVER LIVED

(DE UN CANCIONERO
APÓCRIFO)

1931

⟨∼⟩∼⟨∼⟩∼⟨∼⟩∼⟨∼⟩∼⟨∼⟩∼⟨∼⟩∼⟨∼⟩∼⟨∼⟩∼⟨∼⟩

POEMS FROM THE CIVIL WAR

(POEMAS DE GUERRA)

WRITTEN 1936–39

PUBLISHED AFTER HIS DEATH

Antonio machado published his third book, *Nuevas canciones (New Poems)*, in 1930. Eighteen years had passed since the first version of *Campos de Castilla*, and thirteen years since the enlarged edition. Such patience! Some of those years he spent in Baeza, and then, until 1932, in Segovia. The small room he occupied is still there; his old landlady showed it to me a few years ago.

We notice two advances in *New Poems*. He masters the peculiar union he longed for of introverted subject matter and public form; he brings his substance to the copla form and the folk stanza. The proof of his advance lies in the masterpiece beginning "The huge sea drives / against the flowering mountain." It is one of the most beautiful poems of the twentieth century, derived from a highly developed sensibility, and yet is in no way inaccessible. It resembles in its shape "Thirteen Ways of Looking at a Blackbird."

Machado still believed deeply that the true poem is language caught in time. He developed a sentence he loved to repeat: "Hoy es siempre todavía," which we could translate as "What we are living is a continuation," or "Today is always still," or "There is no separation between past and present," or "Pythagoras and Christ are still alive."

> "I hear old stuff now."
> "Good, sharpen your ears then."

The physicist David Bohm has remarked that when we talk with each other, the words we say are unfolded or explicate, but the meaning of those words is implicate or folded everywhere into the universe. In a similar way, what we experience, instant by instant, appears unfolded, and what has led to this instant also exists, though folded up everywhere in space.

It is as if the past were folded up into the outer world, which Machado goes on struggling to see; and he suggests that if the human being does not learn to see, he will remain a narcissist. Machado mentions in his new series of "Moral Proverbs and Folk Songs" that we are worse off now than in the nineteenth century: the narcissist at that time, associated with the dandy, obsessively looked into a mirroring pond to see his face. The modern narcissist doesn't bother to look in the pond, because he has replaced nature with his own consciousness.

> *This Narcissus of ours*
> *can't see his face in the mirror*
> *because he has become the mirror.*

Machado's disciplined efforts to see bring many original details into his great poem "Passageways." The invention of the stereoscope excited him, and in "Passageways" he tries to bring in both lobes of the brain, as we would say now, and by this double presence create a three-dimensional vision. Heraclitus' praise of lightning comes up in the third poem, and the mystery of the spectrum, of colors that unfold in a certain order, appears in the sixth poem of the series.

Machado wants in his new book first, to see the outer world, and, second, to converse with "the other one who walks by my side." As early as 1908 he had expressed the concept of the "other one" in "Portrait."

> I talk always to the man who walks along with me.

In the second series of "Moral Proverbs and Folk Songs" he writes:

> *Look for your other half*
> *who walks along next to you,*
> *and tends to be what you aren't.*

To find this one, we should look in the mirror, and we will see the other half of us looking back.

Now a wonderfully complicated idea appears: the more we

try to see, the more our "other eyes" can see us. The more we try to see, the more we encourage the "other eyes" to see us.

The eyes you're longing for—
listen now—
the eyes you see yourself in
are eyes because they see you.

This kind of seeing does not make us feel self-conscious, as when we imagine that other people are looking at us, but on the contrary it calms us down, makes us feel seen.

The eye you see is not
an eye because you see it;
it is an eye because it sees you.

Our job is to stitch ourselves and the world together. This is particularly necessary after the appearance in Europe of the Cartesian split by which one usually means the separation of mind and body, or consciousness and world. A gap develops between the westerner and the world, and he falls in. It is as if the western man or woman sees, but nothing looks back.

I notice also in this book a powerful advance in thinking. If Antonio Machado in *Campos de Castilla* invited thinking to enter the poem, we could say that he takes a further step now, and invites philosophical thinking to enter. He is not afraid that it will kill feeling, and it doesn't.

To do philosophical thinking implies that one takes the old philosophical arguments seriously, as if the old philosophers were still alive, and then one takes a stand on them. "With old Heraclitus we believe that the world is ruled by lightning."

Machado takes up several philosophical problems, and one is this: If God is absolute Being, then how could He have created, in us and the world, something incomplete? It can also be put this way: Since creation, like thought, always proceeds by opposites, then God, who is absolute Being, would of course create absolute Nothing, or Nada. But the world partially at least exists, so there we are again. Verlaine expressed the paradox, saying: "The universe amounts to a flaw /

in the purity of non-existence." The medium Michael Mac-Macha once said to me that this idea is the essence of the insanity that the Aryans brought down with them from the mountains around 1500 B.C.—in its accent on purity it is a little insane. And I like it that Machado when he thinks does not reject this philosophical problem passed on to us by the Aryan past, but instead takes it in his arms; one could say that if these old problems are old clothes, he washes them. He brings the problems down to the river, and spends years washing them.

The washing he does in two places: the new series of "Moral Proverbs and Folk Songs" (I have translated forty of the ninety-nine in the series) and in the "Abel Martín" poems.

"Moral Proverbs and Folk Songs," with swift thinking and elegant poetry mingled, is a genre Machado invented. The genre derives from four distinct models. One is the popular Spanish copla, the second the sayings of Pythagoras, the third the Japanese haiku, and the fourth the wisdom quatrains of Moslem and Jewish literature. Machado refers several times to Sem Tob, the fourteenth-century doctor and rabbi whose book of seven hundred quatrains he read. Machado points out that not-thinking is no guarantee that you exist:

> *Now someone has come up with this:*
> Cogito ergo non sum.
> *What an exaggeration!*

But his late masterpieces are the "Abel Martín" poems. Abel Martín, his invented poet-philosopher, helped him to say certain things, and he composed for Abel Martín a small book of about sixty pages, made up of literary criticism, remembrances of Martín by his student Juan de Mairena, poems by both men, and commentary on the philosophical implications of these poems. "In the theology of Abel Martín," Mairena says, "God is defined as absolute Being, and therefore nothing which exists could be his work."

> *When the* I AM THAT I AM *made nothing*
> *and rested, which rest it certainly deserved,*

night now accompanied day, and man
had his friend in the absence of the woman.

Nada, or Pure Nothing, Machado imagines in this poem as
the zero or empty egg. Reason, which is able to abstract, and
so approach this empty circle, now appears, or breaks out, in
man.

And the universal egg rose, empty,
pale, chill and not yet heavy with matter,
full of unweighable mist, in his hand.

Only the "standing animals" can see zero, and so only they are
capable of conceptual thought, on the one hand, or "olvido"
on the other, which literally means "forgetting," but which
implies letting something fall out of the conscious mind.

Since the wild animal's back is now your shoulder,
and since the miracle of not-being is finished,
start then, poet, a song at the edge of it all
to death, to silence, and to what does not return.

"Siesta," Juan de Mairena's elegy for Abel Martin, I think is
one of the most powerful brief poems of the century. So much
of Machado returns here: time passing returns as the goldfish,
the Roman and Greek past returns as Cupid, who "flies away
in the white stone," art that is accessible returns as the ivory
copla of the green cicada, and God's creation of nothing
returns as the siesta, which amounts to a short time of silence
in the midst of noise.

let us give honor to the Lord—
the black mark of his good hand—
who has arranged for silence in all this noise.

Faith does not give birth to human thought, but human
thought is hidden inside faith, as a sculpture is hidden inside
a block of stone.

Honor to the God of distance and of absence,
of the anchor in the sea—the open sea—
He frees us from the world—it's everywhere—
He opens roads for us to walk on.

Because "Hoy es siempre todavía," all that has lived is still living. Machado is now in his fifties, but his childhood is still within him, perhaps even events that took place before he was born. I'll end my commentary on his work with a memory he let Juan de Mairena tell.

Another incident, also important, took place before I was born. There were some dolphins who lost their way, and riding the tides, ascended the Guadalquiver River, arriving at least as far up as Seville. People came down to the river from all over the city, drawn by the extraordinary sight, young girls, lovers, and among them my parents, who wanted to see this sight they had never seen. It was a bright afternoon. I recall that afternoon now and then . . . or perhaps I imagined it or dreamt it.

NEW POEMS

⌒⌒⌒⌒⌒⌒⌒⌒⌒⌒⌒⌒⌒⌒⌒⌒⌒⌒⌒⌒⌒⌒

THE COLLECTED WORKS OF A
POET WHO NEVER LIVED

⌒⌒⌒⌒⌒⌒⌒⌒⌒⌒⌒⌒⌒⌒⌒⌒⌒⌒⌒⌒⌒⌒

POEMS FROM THE CIVIL WAR

GALERÍAS

I

En el azul la banda
de unos pájaros negros
que chillan, aletean y se posan
en el álamo yerto.
. . . En el desnudo álamo,
las graves chovas quietas y en silencio,
cual negras, frías notas
escritas en la pauta de febrero.

II

El monte azul, el río, las erectas
varas cobrizas de los finos álamos,
y el blanco del almendro en la colina,
¡oh nieve en flor y mariposa en árbol!
Con el aroma del habar, el viento
corre en la alegre soledad del campo.

III

Una centella blanca
en la nube de plomo culebrea.
¡Los asombrados ojos
del niño, y juntas cejas
—está el salón oscuro—de la madre!. . .
¡Oh cerrado balcón a la tormenta!
El viento aborrascado y el granizo
en el limpio cristal repiquetean.

PASSAGEWAYS

1

Against the blue sky,
birds, black, a flight—
they cry, wallop their wings, and settle
in a stark poplar.
. . . The sober jackdaws
motionless, silent, in the bare poplar
are cold black notes
copied out on February staves.

2

The blue mountain, the river, the firm
coppery twigs on the slender poplars,
and the white of the almond tree on the hill!
Oh snow in the blossom and the butterfly in the tree!
Carrying the aroma of the bean fields, the wind
runs through the joyful solitude of the fields!

3

A white lightning bolt
snakes down the lead-colored cloud.
The boy's big startled
eyes—the room is dark—
the mother's eyebrows joining!
Oh balcony doors well closed to the storm!
The harsh wind gusts and the grains of hail
drum again and again on the clean pane.

IV

El iris y el balcón. Las siete cuerdas
de la lira del sol vibran en sueños.
Un tímpano infantil da siete golpes
—agua y cristal—. Acacias con jilgueros
Cigüeñas en las torres. En la plaza,
lavó la lluvia el mirto polvoriento.
En el amplio rectángulo ¿quién puso
ese grupo de vírgenes risueño,
y arriba ¡hosanna! entre la rota nube,
la palma de oro y el azul sereno?

V

Entre montes de almagre y peñas grises
el tren devora su raíl de acero.
La hilera de brillantes ventanillas
lleva un doble perfil de camafeo,
tras el cristal de plata, repetido . . .
¿Quién ha punzado el corazón del tiempo?

VI

¿Quién puso, entre las rocas de ceniza,
para la miel del sueño,
esas retamas de oro
y esas azules flores del romero?
La sierra de violeta
y, en el poniente, el azafrán del cielo,
¿quién ha pintado? ¡El abejar, la ermita.
el tajo sobre el río, el sempiterno
rodar del agua entre las hondas peñas,
y el rubio verde de los campos nuevos,
y todo, hasta la tierra blanca y rosa
al pie de los almendros!

4

The balcony and the rainbow.
                    The sun's lyre,
that has seven strings, resonates in dreams.
A childlike drum gives seven strokes—
rain and windowpane—
                    Acacias and finches.
Storks on the towers.
                    Rain fallen
in the plaza has washed the dusty myrtle trees.
And the ample square—who has placed
there that smiling group of virgins?
And higher up—hosanna!—a break in the clouds,
the palm branch of gold and the calm blue!

5

Going between heaps of grey rocks and ochre earth,
the train eats up its steel rails.
The row of train windows that reflect sunlight
carries profiles, as on a cameo, but double,
behind the silver glass, more and more appear. . . .
Who pierced the heart of time?

6

Who placed there among the cindery rocks,
for the beehive of dreams,
these yellow furze blossoms,
and these blue rosemarys?
Who painted the mountains
violet, and the sky saffron
far to the west? The hive, the hermit's hut,
the saddleback over the river, the eternal
water sound below the high boulders,
and the lemony green of the new oats,
all of it—even the ground white and rosy
around the trunk of the almonds!

En el silencio sigue
la lira pitagórica vibrando,
el iris en la luz, la luz que llena
mi estereoscopio vano.
Han cegado mis ojos las cenizas
del fuego heraclitano.
El mundo es, un momento,
transparente, vacío, ciego, alado.

7

The harp of Pythagoras goes on
resonating in the silence,
the rainbow resonates in the sunlight, the same light that
    enters
the stereoscope I can't quite master.
The ashes left from Heraclitus'
fire have put out my eyes.
The whole world this instant
is transparent, empty, blind, flying.

IRIS DE LA NOCHE

A D. Ramón del Valle-Inclán

Hacia Madrid, una noche,
va el tren por el Guadarrama.
En el cielo, el arco iris
que hacen la luna y el agua.
¡Oh luna de abril, serena,
que empuja las nubes blancas!
La madre lleva a su niño,
dormido, sobre la falda.
Duerme el niño y, todavía,
ve el campo verde que pasa,
y arbolillos soleados,
y mariposas doradas.
La madre, ceño sombrío
entre un ayer y un mañana,
ve unas ascuas mortecinas
y una hornilla con arañas.
Hay un trágico viajero,
que debe ver cosas raras,
y habla solo y, cuando mira,
nos borra con la mirada.
Yo pienso en campos de nieve
y en pinos de otras montañas.
Y tú, Señor, por quien todos
vemos y que ves las almas,
dinos si todos, un día,
hemos de verte la cara.

RAINBOW AT NIGHT

for Don Ramón del Valle-Inclán

The train moves through the Guadarrama
one night on the way to Madrid.
The moon and the fog create
high up a rainbow.
Oh April moon, so calm,
driving the white clouds!

The mother holds her boy
sleeping on her lap.
The boy sleeps, and nevertheless
sees the green fields outside,
and trees lit up by sun,
and the golden butterflies.

The mother, her forehead dark
between a day gone and a day to come,
sees a fire nearly out
and an oven with spiders.

There's a traveler mad with grief,
no doubt seeing odd things;
he talks to himself, and when he looks
wipes us out with his look.

I remember fields under snow,
and pine trees of other mountains.

And you, Lord, through whom we all
have eyes, and who sees souls,
tell us if we all one
day will see your face.

CANCIONES

I

Junto a la sierra florida,
bulle el ancho mar.
El panal de mis abejas
tiene granitos de sal.

II

Junto al agua negra.
Olor de mar y jazmines.
Noche malagueña.

III

La primavera ha venido.
Nadie sabe cómo ha sido.

IV

La primavera ha venido.
¡Aleluyas blancas
de los zarzales floridos!

V

¡Luna llena, luna llena,
tan oronda, tan redonda
en esta noche serena
de marzo, panal de luz
que labran blancas abejas!

VI

Noche castellana;
la canción se dice,
o, mejor, se calla.
Cuando duerman todos,
saldré a la ventana.

SONGS

I

The huge sea drives
against the flowering mountain.
The comb of my honeybees
holds tiny grains of salt.

II

Not far from the black water.
Odor of the sea and of jasmine flowers.
Night of Málaga.

III

The spring has arrived.
No one knows what happened.

IV

The spring has arrived.
Snow-white hallelujahs
from the flowering blackberry bushes!

V

Full moon, full moon,
so great, so round
in this tranquil night
of March, honeycomb of light
that the white bees have made!

VI

Night of Castille;
the poem is spoken,
or, better, not spoken.
When everyone is sleeping,
I'll go to the window.

VII

Canta, canta en claro rimo,
el almendro en verde rama
y el doble sauce del río.

Canta de la parda encina
la rama que el hacha corta,
y la flor que nadie mira.

De los perales del huerto
la blanca flor, la rosada
flor del melocotonero.

Y este olor
que arranca el viento mojado
a los habares en flor.

VIII

La fuente y las cuatro
acacias en flor
de la plazoleta.
Ya no quema el sol.
¡Tardecita alegre!
Canta, ruiseñor.
Es la misma hora
de mi corazón.

IX

¡Blanca hospedería,
celda de viajero,
con la sombra mía!

X

El acueducto romano
— canta una voz de mi tierra —
y el querer que nos tenemos,
chiquilla, ¡vaya firmeza!

VII

Sing, sing in crisp sound
the almond tree leafed out,
and the double willows by the river.

Sing of the ordinary oak,
the branch cut off by the ax,
and the flower no one looks at.

And the white blossom
on the pear tree, the rosy
flower of the peach tree.

And this perfume
which the damp wind is pulling
from the blossoming bean patch.

VIII

The fountain and the four
acacias in flower
in the garden.
The sun doesn't burn now.
Wonderful dusk!
Nightingale, sing.
The same hour has come
inside my body.

IX

White inn,
the traveler's room,
with my shadow!

X

"The Roman aqueduct"
—murmurs a voice in my dialect—
"and the love we have for each other,
my darling, there is steadiness!"

XI
A las palabras de amor
les sienta bien su poquito
de exageración.

XII
En Santo Domingo,
la misa mayor.
Aunque me decían
hereje y masón,
rezando contigo,
¡cuánta devoción!

XIII
Hay fiesta en el prado verde
— pífano y tambor —.
Con su cayado florido
y abarcas de oro vino un pastor.

Del monte bajé,
sólo por bailar con ella;
al monte me tornaré.

En los árboles del huerto
hay un ruiseñor;
canta de noche y de día,
canta a la luna y al sol.

Ronco de cantar:
al huerto vendrá la niña
y una rosa cortará.

Entre las negras encinas,
hay una fuente de piedra,
y un cantarillo de barro
que nunca se llena.

Por el encinar,
con la blanca luna,
ella volverá.

In words of love
a tiny bit of exaggeration
feels right.

High mass
in Santo Domingo.
Though they call me
heretic and Mason,
praying with you,
what devotion!

There is a fiesta in the green field
—fife and drum.
With his flowery shepherd crook
and gold sandals a shepherd came.

I came down from the mountain,
solely to dance with her;
and I'll return to the mountain.

There is a nightingale
in the garden trees;
it sings night and day,
it sings to the moon and the sun.
Hoarse from singing, it sings;
the girl will come to the garden
and pick a rose.

Among the black oaks
there is a stone fountain,
and a tiny jug of clay there
which never gets full.

She will return
through the black oaks
when the white moon comes out.

Contigo en Valonsadero,
fiesta de San Juan,
mañana en la Pampa,
del otro lado del mar.
Guárdame la fe,
que yo volveré.

Mañana seré pampero,
y se me irá el corazón
a orillas del Alto Duero.

XV

Mientras danzáis en corro,
niñas, cantad:
Ya están los prados verdes,
ya vino abril galán.

A la orilla del río,
por el negro encinar,
sus abarcas de plata
hemos visto brillar.
Ya están los prados verdes,
ya vino abril galán.

With you in Valonsadero,
fiesta of St. John,
tomorrow to Argentina
on the other side of the sea.
Keep believing in me,
for I will return.

Tomorrow I'll be a ranchero,
and my heart will go
to the banks of the high Duero.

While you are dancing in a ring,
girls, sing:
Now the fields are green,
now bonny April has come.

Along the riverbank
by the black oaks,
we have watched his silvery
sandals flash.
Now the fields are green,
now handsome April has come.

PROVERBIOS Y CANTARES

A José Ortega y Gasset

I

El ojo que ves no es
ojo porque tú lo veas;
es ojo porque te ve.

II

Para dialogar,
preguntad primero;
después . . . escuchad.

III

Todo narcisismo
es un vicio feo,
y ya viejo vicio.

IV

Mas busca en tu espejo al otro,
al otro que va contigo.

V

Entre el vivir y el soñar
hay una tercera cosa.
Adivínala.

VI

Ese tu Narciso
ya no se ve en el espejo
porque es el espejo mismo.

FORTY POEMS CHOSEN FROM "MORAL PROVERBS AND FOLK SONGS"

Dedicated to José Ortega y Gasset

I

The eye you see is not
an eye because you see it;
it is an eye because it sees you.

II

To talk with someone,
ask a question first,
then—listen.

III

Narcissism
is an ugly fault,
and now it's a boring fault too.

IV

But look in your mirror for the other one,
the other one who walks by your side.

V

Between living and dreaming
there is a third thing.
Guess it.

VI

This Narcissus of ours
can't see his face in the mirror
because he has become the mirror.

VII

¿Siglo nuevo? ¿Todavía
llamea la misma fragua?
¿Corre todavía el agua
por el cauce que tenía?

VIII

Hoy es siempre todavía.

IX

Sol en Aries. Mi ventana
está abierta al aire frío.
— ¡Oh rumor de agua lejana! —
La tarde despierta al río.

X

En el viejo caserío
— ¡oh anchas torres con cigüeñas! —,
enmudece el son gregario,
y en el campo solitario
suena el agua entre las peñas.

XI

Como otra vez, mi atención
está del agua cautiva;
pero del agua en la viva
roca de mi corazón.

XII

¿Sabes, cuando el agua suena,
si es agua de cumbre o valle,
de plaza, jardín o huerta?

XIII

Encuentro lo que no busco:
las hojas del toronjil
huelen a limón maduro.

VII

New century? Still
firing up the same forge?
Is the water still going along in its bed?

VIII

Every instant is Still.

IX

The sun in Aries. My window
is open to the cool air.
Oh the sound of the water far off!
The evening awakens the river.

X

In the old farmhouse
—a high tower with storks!—
the gregarious sound falls silent,
and in the field where no one is,
water makes a sound among the rocks.

XI

Just as before, I'm interested
in water held in;
but now water in the living
rock of my chest.

XII

When you hear water, does its sound tell you
if it's from mountain or farm,
city street, formal garden, or orchard?

XIII

What I find surprises me:
leaves of the garden balm
smell of lemonwood.

XIV

Nunca traces tu frontera,
ni cuides de tu perfil;
todo eso es cosa de fuera.

XV

Busca a tu complementario,
que marcha siempre contigo,
y suele ser tu contrario.

XVI

Si vino la primavera,
volad a las flores;
no chupéis cera.

XVII

En mi soledad
he visto cosas muy claras,
que no son verdad.

XVIII

Buena es el agua y la sed;
buena es la sombra y el sol;
la miel de flor de romero,
la miel de campo sin flor.

XIX

Sólo quede un símbolo:
quod elixum est ne asato.
No aséis lo que está cocido.

XX

Canta, canta, canta,
junto a su tomate,
el grillo en su jaula.

XIV

Don't trace out your profile,
forget your side view—
all that is outer stuff.

XV

Look for your other half
who walks always next to you
and tends to be what you aren't.

XVI

When spring comes,
go to the flowers—
why keep on sucking wax?

XVII

In my solitude
I have seen things very clearly
that were not true.

XVIII

Water is good, so is thirst;
shadow is good, so is sun;
the honey from the rosemarys
and the honey of the bare fields.

XIX

Only one creed stands:
quod elixum est ne asato.
Don't roast what's already boiled.

XX

Sing on, sing on, sing on,
the cricket in his cage
near his darling tomato.

XXI

Despacito y buena letra:
el hacer las cosas bien
importa más que el hacerlas.

XXII

Sin embargo...
                        ¡Ah!, sin embargo,
importa avivar los remos,
dijo el caracol al galgo.

XXIII

¡Ya hay hombres activos!
Soñaba la charca
con sus mosquitos.

XXIV

Despertad, cantores:
acaben los ecos,
empiecen las voces.

XXV

Mas no busquéis disonancias;
porque, al fin, nada disuena,
siempre al son que tocan bailan.

XXVI

No es el yo fundamental
eso que busca el poeta,
sino el tú esencial.

XXVII

Los ojos por que suspiras,
sábelo bien,
los ojos en que te miras
son ojos porque te ven.

XXI

Form your letters slowly and well:
making things well
is more important than making them.

XXII

All the same . . .

               Ah yes! All the same,
moving the legs fast is important,
as the snail said to the greyhound.

XXIII

There are really men of action now!
The marsh was dreaming
of its mosquitoes.

XXIV

Wake up, you poets:
let echoes end,
and voices begin.

XXV

But don't hunt for dissonance;
because, in the end, there is no dissonance.
When the sound is heard people dance.

XXVI

What the poet is searching for
is not the fundamental I
but the deep you.

XXVII

The eyes you're longing for—
listen now—
the eyes you see yourself in
are eyes because they see you.

XXVIII

Tras el vivir y el soñar,
está lo que más importa:
despertar.

XXIX

Ya hubo quien pensó:
cogito ergo non sum.
¡Qué exageración!

XXX

Creí mi hogar apagado,
y revolví la ceniza . . .
Me quemé la mano.

XXXI

Poned atención:
un corazón solitario
no es un corazón.

XXXII

Lo ha visto pasar en sueños . . .
Buen cazador de sí mismo,
siempre en acecho.

XXXIII

Cazó a su hombre malo,
el de los días azules,
siempre cabizbajo.

XXXIV

Mas no te importe si rueda
y pasa de mano en mano:
del oro se hace moneda.

XXVIII

Beyond living and dreaming
there is something more important:
waking up.

XXIX

Now someone has come up with this!
Cogito ergo non sum.
What an exaggeration!

XXX

I thought my fire was out,
and stirred the ashes. . . .
I burnt my fingers.

XXXI

Pay attention now:
a heart that's all by itself
is not a heart.

XXXII

I've caught a glimpse of him in dreams:
expert hunter of himself,
every minute in ambush.

XXXIII

He caught his bad man:
the one who on sunny days
walks with head down.

XXXIV

If a poem becomes common,
passed around, hand to hand, it's OK:
gold is chosen for coins.

XXXV
Si vivir es bueno,
es mejor soñar,
y mejor que todo,
madre, despertar.

XXXVI
No el sol, sino la campana,
cuando te despierta, es
lo mejor de la mañana.

XXXVII
Entre las brevas soy blando;
entre las rocas, de piedra.
¡Malo!

XXXVIII
Tengo a mis amigos
en mi soledad;
cuando estoy con ellos
¡qué lejos están!

XXXIX
Tu profecía, poeta.
—Mañana hablarán los mudos:
el corazón y la piedra.

XL
—¿ Mas el arte?...
                              —Es puro juego,
que es igual a pura vida,
que es igual a puro fuego,
Veréis el ascua encendida.

[152]

XXXV

If it's good to live,
then it's better to be asleep dreaming,
and best of all,
mother, is to awake.

XXXVI

Sunlight is good for waking,
but I prefer bells—
the best thing about morning.

XXXVII

Among the figs I am soft,
Among the rocks I am hard.
That's bad!

XXXVIII

When I am alone
how close my friends are;
when I am with them
how distant they are!

XXXIX

Now, poet, your prophecy?
"Tomorrow what is dumb will speak,
the human heart and the stone."

XL

But art?
It is pure and intense play,
so it is like pure and intense life,
so it is like pure and intense fire.
You'll see the coal burning.

AL GRAN CERO

Cuando el *Ser que se es* hizo la nada
y reposó, que bien lo merecía,
ya tuvo el día noche, y compañía
tuvo el hombre en la ausencia de la amada.

Fiat umbra! Brotó el pensar humano.
Y el huevo universal alzó, vacío,
ya sin color, desustanciado y frío,
lleno de niebla ingrávida, en su mano.

Toma el cero integral, la hueca esfera,
que has de mirar, si lo has de ver, erguido.
Hoy que es espalda el lomo de tu fiera,

y es el milagro del no ser cumplido,
brinda, poeta, un canto de frontera
a la muerte, al silencio y al olvido.

TO THE GREAT CIRCLE OF NOTHING

When the I AM THAT I AM made nothing
and rested, which rest it certainly deserved,
night now accompanied day, and man
had his friend in the absence of the woman.

Let there be shadow! Human thinking broke out.
And the universal egg rose, empty,
pale, chill and not yet heavy with matter,
full of unweighable mist, in his hand.

Take the numerical zero, the sphere with nothing in it:
it has to be seen, if you have to see it, standing.
Since the wild animal's back now is your shoulder,

and since the miracle of not-being is finished,
start then, poet, a song at the edge of it all
to death, to silence, and to what does not return.

ÚLTIMAS LAMENTACIONES DE ABEL MARTÍN

(Cancionero apócrifo)

Hoy, con la primavera,
soñé que un fino cuerpo me seguía
cual dócil sombrá. Era
mi cuerpo juvenil, el que subía
de tres en tres peldaños la escalera.
—Hola, galgo de ayer. (Su luz de acuario
trocaba el hondo espejo
por agria luz sobre un rincón de osario.)
—¿Tú conmigo, rapaz?
              —Contigo, viejo.
Soñé la galería
al huerto de ciprés y limonero;
tibias palomas en la piedra fría,
en el cieló de añil rojo pandero.
y en la mágica angustia de la infancia
la vigilia del ángel más austero.
La ausencia y la distancia
volví a soñar con túnicas de aurora;
firme en el arco tenso la saeta
del mañana, la vista aterradora
de la llama prendida en la espoleta
de su granada.
            ¡Oh Tiempo, oh Todavía
preñado de inminencias!
Tú me acompañas en la senda fría,
tejedor de esperanzas e impaciencias.

*

¡El tiempo y sus banderas desplegadas!
(¿Yo, capitán? Mas yo no voy contigo.)
¡Hacia lejanas torres soleadas
el perdurable asalto por castigo!

ABEL MARTÍN'S LAST LAMENTATIONS

Today it was spring;
I dreamt that a slender body followed me
like an obedient shadow. It was
my boyish body, the one who used to leap
the stairs three at a time.
"Hello there, old runner!" (The deep mirror
altered the aquarium light
to a harsh light over the bone yard.)
"Are you with me, speedy?"
                                    "With you, old man."
Then I seemed to see the rows
of cypress and lemon trees in the garden;
chill cobblestones with warm pigeons,
and the red kite high in the blue sky,
and some stern angel who watched
over the magic anguish of childhood.
Everything distant and disappeared
came back, as I dreamed, as fresh as dawn;
in the bow drawn back, firm, the arrow
of tomorrow, the terrifying sight
of the flame that is moving in the fuse
toward its charge. . . .
                        Oh Time, the past still present,
pregnant with all about to come,
you walk with me on the cold path,
weaver of the threads of hope and impatience!

*

Time and its flags blowing in the wind!
(Me, Captain? But I'm not going along.)
Sent out for punishment to attack constantly
the sunlit towers far in the distance!

Hoy, como un día, en la ancha mar violeta
hunde el sueño su pétrea escalinata,
y hace camino la infantil goleta,
y le salta el delfín de bronce y plata.
La hazaña y la aventura
cercando un corazón entelerido . . .
Montes de piedra dura
—eco y eco—mi voz han repetido.

¡Oh, descansar en el azul del día
como descansa el águila en el viento,
sobre la sierra fría,
segura de sus alas y su aliento!
La augusta confianza
a ti, Naturaleza, y paz te pido,
mi tregua de temor y de esperanza,
un grano de alegría, un mar de olvido . . .

*

Today as once before, the dream lets down its stone
stairs into the deep and violet ocean,
and the child's sailboat makes its way
as the dolphin of silver and bronze leaps out.

Heroic acts and adventures
hover around the fearful soul. . . .
Cliffs of impenetrable rock
send back my voice—echo after echo.

How marvellous to lie back on the blue air,
as the eagle lies back on the wind,
over the cold peaks,
certain of his wings and his breath!

What I ask from you, Nature,
is a deeply interfused confidence and peace,
a reprieve from fear and from hope
a sand grain of joy, an ocean of oblivion . . .

SIESTA

En memoria de Abel Martín

Mientras traza su curva el pez de fuego,
junto al ciprés, bajo el supremo añil,
y vuela en blanca piedra el niño ciego,
y en el olmo la copla de marfil
de la verde cigarra late y suena,
honremos al Señor
—la negra estampa de su mano buena—
que ha dictado el silencio en el clamor.

Al dios de la distancia y de la ausencia,
del áncora en el mar, la plena mar...
Él nos libra del mundo—omnipresencia—,
nos abre senda para caminar.

Con la copa de sombra bien colmada,
con este nunca lleno corazón,
honremos al Señor que hizo la Nada
y ha esculpido en la fe nuestra razón.

SIESTA

In Memory of Abel Martín

While the burning fish is tracing his arc
near the cypress, beneath the highest blue of all,
and the blind boy flies away in the white stone,
and the ivory poem of the green cicada
beats and reverberates in the elm,
let us give honor to the Lord—
the black mark of his good hand—
who has arranged for silence in all this noise.

Honor to the god of distance and of absence,
of the anchor in the sea—the open sea . . .
He frees us from the world—it's everywhere—
he opens roads for us to walk on.

With our cup of darkness filled to the brim,
with our heart that always knows some hunger,
let us give honor to the Lord who created the zero
and carved our thought out of the block of faith.

LA MUERTE DEL NIÑO HERIDO

Otra vez es la noche . . . Es el martillo
de la fiebre en las sienes bien vendadas
del niño. —Madre ¡el pájaro amarillo!
¡las mariposas negras y moradas!

—Duerme, hijo mío—. Y la manita oprime
la madre junto al lecho. —¡Oh flor de fuego!
¿Quién ha de helarte, flor de sangre, dime?
Hay en la pobre alcoba olor de espliego;

fuera, la oronda luna que blanquea
cúpula y torre a la ciudad sombría.
Invisible avión moscardonea.

—¿Duermes, oh dulce flor de sangre mía?
El cristal del balcón repiquetea.
—¡Oh, fría, fría, fría, fría, fría!

THE DEATH OF THE WOUNDED CHILD

In the night once more . . . It is the fever-
hammer in the bandaged temples
of the boy. "Mother! The yellow bird!
The butterflies are black and purple!"

"Sleep, my son." The mother by the bed
squeezes the tiny hand. "My burning flower,
my bloodflower, who freezes you? Tell me!"
There is an odor of lavender in the stark bedroom;

outside the swollen moon is turning white
the cupola and steeple of the darkened city.
An invisible aeroplane hums.

"Are you asleep, sweet flower of my blood?"
The pane on the balcony window shivers.
"Oh cold, cold, cold, cold, cold."

COPLAS

En los yermos altos
veo unos chopos de frío
y un camino blanco.

*

En aquella piedra
(¡tierras de la luna!)
¿nadie lo recuerda?

*

Azotan el limonar
las ráfagas de febrero.
No duermo por no soñar.

COPLAS

In the high wilderness
I see some cold poplars
and a white road.

*

In that stony place—
(landscape of the moon!)
does no one remember it?

*

The gusts of February
rip through the lemon trees.
I don't sleep so I won't dream.

MEDITACIÓN DEL DÍA

Frente a la palma de fuego
que deja el sol que se va,
en la tarde silenciosa
y en este jardín de paz,
mientras Valencia florida
se bebe el Guadalaviar
—Valencia de finas torres,
en el lírico cielo de Ausias March,
trocando su río en rosas
antes que llegue a la mar—,
pienso en la guerra. La guerra
viene como un huracán
por los páramas del alto Duero,
por las llanuras de pan llevar,
desde la fértil Extremadura
a estos jardines de limonar,
desde los grises cielos astures
a las marismas de luz y sal.
Pienso en España vendida toda
de río a río, de monte a monte, de mar a mar.

TODAY'S MEDITATION

The fiery palm tree in front of me,
that the setting sun is just now leaving,
this late and silent afternoon,
inside our peaceful garden,
while flowery old Valencia
drinks the Guadalaviar waters—
Valencia of delicate towers,
in the joyful sky of Ausias March,
her river turns entirely into roses
before it arrives at the sea—
I think of the war. The war
is like a tornado moving
through the bleak foothills of the Duero,
through the plains of standing wheat,
from the farmlands of Extremadura
to these gardens with private lemons,
from the grey skies of the north
to these salty marshes full of light.
I think of Spain, all of it sold out,
river by river, mountain by mountain, sea to sea.

AFTERWORD

AN HOMAGE TO MACHADO IN 1966

A DAY set aside to honor Antonio Machado, the great Spanish poet who died in exile in southern France in 1939, had been announced for the 20th of February 1966. The homage, notice of which was given all government bureaus concerned, was to consist of the unveiling of a monument to Machado—a bronze head made by the sculptor Pablo Serrono. The bust would be unveiled in the town of Baeza (Jaén Province), where Machado had taught French for several years in the local school; the monument was to be placed at a spot outside town, a particularly lovely spot often visited by Machado in his walks. The homage was announced under the title "Walks with Antonio Machado."

The committee that organized it was heterogeneous, including the judge in Baeza as well as many writers and artists living in Madrid. The Spanish press gave considerable publicity to the plans for the homage. Several days before it, the weekly *Triunfo* in Madrid published a full-page photograph of the bronze bust, now finished, as illustration to an article written by Moreno Galván; at the same time a number of papers published declarations of support for the homage, plus various other testimonies of public sympathy for the project.

The day before the homage, a brief note appeared in several papers, its origin unknown, declaring that the homage had been canceled. By that time, most of the people who had intended to be there were already on the way from various parts of Spain—from Alicante, Seville, Córdoba, Valencia, Barcelona, Bilbao, Madrid. . . .

The Guardia Civil, armed with submachine guns, waited for the cars on all the roads around Baeza, several kilometers from the city limits. They stopped all buses, but let private cars go through, at least in the beginning, though not without noting down the license numbers. Many people walked into town from that spot later, when private cars were halted.

Under these circumstances some 2,500 people arrived in Baeza on the twentieth, not counting another large group that did not succeed in breaking through the police line. The daily paper *Jaén* declared: "Today Baeza will render an homage to Machado." The crowd of people moved out of town toward the area of the monument. The line was long and silent, but the mood was a mood of affection and camaraderie among the admirers of the poet. Shortly before the line arrived at the spot, some Armed Police (popularly called "the Greys" because of their uniform) appeared and blocked the road. Several participants walked forward to ask for an explanation, which the police refused. A lieutenant arrived, and soon police reinforcements. There was great tension. The police lieutenant said flatly that the gathering was canceled, and that they had orders to keep people away from the place in question. He said he did not know the reasons why. He was asked to make known to some authority—the mayor of the city or the governor of the province—the unanimous desire of those present that some explanation be given them for what was taking place. The lieutenant refused this and threatened to charge the group. Those present pressed together in lines and made known their decision to wait there for the arrival of someone in power who would give them a good explanation. The effort these people had gone through to get here, many from places far away, should not be made to end in a simple return home under the arbitrary order of some member of the state police or an official of the constabulary.

The lieutenant took a step backward and blew a whistle. The police drew up in lines and took out their clubs. The lieutenant read a paragraph referring to "violations of the laws of Public Order" and announced that at the third blow of the whistle, the police "would charge" against persons present. Those present linked arms tightly, prepared to hold to their decision to wait for a decent explanation of the cancellation.

The charge began. The Greys held back a moment. The officer drew his pistol and shouted, "Charge! Charge!" A policeman, also from the Political-Social Brigade, waved his pistol as if he were fencing, furious, absolutely out of his mind. "Charge! Charge!"

From then on it was brutality and violence. The crowd cried: "Murderer! Murderer!" Many fell down under the blows. Groans, cries; young people sobbed with fear. The Greys savagely pursued the few people who ran in the first moments, and continued to beat those who remained standing, both those facing the police and those trying to help others on the ground.

The large mass of people, after returning two kilometers, back to town, filed into the main plaza of Baeza in a mood of rage, exasperation and fear. Some took shelter in bars or cafés, from which the police expelled them by force, back to the street, where they were met with more violence; blows, insults and various indignities. Many arrests took place and the tracking began—the pursuit of people into every nook of town: new arrests and high-handedness.

The town watched this sight astonished. "Get to your cars!" the Greys shouted, pushing heavily against anyone and everyone. The deputies from the Political Social Brigade assisted them on all sides. Those who had no cars to leave town with were thwacked, chased, hunted into any shelter they could take. A long parade of cars fled by all the highways leading out, and those who arrived in Ubeda (a nearby town) could see the officers in the Guardia Civil barracks waiting for the order to go to Baeza.

This is what happened to the homage for Antonio Machado in Baeza the 20th of February 1966.

Twenty-seven people were arrested, among them José Moreno Galván (author of the article mentioned above); Pedro Caba (doctor); Eduardo Urculo (painter); Manuel

Aguilar (publisher); Roberto Puig (architect); Cortijo (painter); Ripollés (painter); Alfredo Flores (lawyer); J. A. Rámos Herranz (engineer); Pedro Dicenta (teacher); Carlos Álvarez (poet), etc.

Of the twenty-seven arrested, sixteen were released just before dawn. Eleven remained in jail, and were taken to Jaén and released there the next day, after they had paid fines varying according to the case from 5,000 pesetas to 10,000, 15,000 and 25,000 pesetas.

The report of an eyewitness
Translated from the Spanish by Robert Bly

TRANSLATIONS OF MACHADO
AVAILABLE IN ENGLISH

Barnstone, Willis. *The Dream Below the Sun*. Trumansberg, N.Y.: The Crossing Press, 1981. A reissue, with many additional poems, of next entry.

———. *Eighty Poems of Antonio Machado*. New York: Las Americas, 1959. Includes Juan Ramon Jimenez' reminiscence of Machado.

Craige, Betty Jean. *Selected Poems of Antonio Machado*. Baton Rouge: Louisiana State University Press, 1978. Highly academic.

Falck, Colin. *The Garden in the Evening*. 14 poems. Oxford, England: *The Review*, No. 13, 1965.

Rexroth, Kenneth. *Thirty Spanish Poems of Love and Exile*. San Francisco: City Lights, 1955. Several brilliant translations.

Scholes, Carmen, and William Witherup. *I Go Dreaming Roads*. 22 poems. Monterey, Ca.: Peters Gate Press, 1973.

Trueblood, Alan S. *Antonio Machado: Selected Poems*. Cambridge, Ma.: Harvard University Press, 1982. A generous selection, sixty-four poems, with marvelous notes.

Times Alone has been composed in Linotype Baskerville and printed on 60 pound Warren's Olde Style by Heritage Printers, Inc., and bound by The Delmar Company.

Designed by Joyce Kachergis.

Wesleyan University Press, 1983.

Robert Bly is the author of ten books of poetry. Antonio Machado was a strong influence on his first book of poetry, *Silence in the Snowy Fields*. Bly has edited and translated works of Swedish, German, Norwegian, and Persian poetry, including that of Neruba and Rilke. He received the National Book Award for poetry in 1968. His home is in Moose Lake, Minnesota.

5/30/02